More Than 100 Grain-Free, Dairy-Free Recipes for Wholesome, Delicious Bread

The

PALEO BREAD BIBLE

ANNA CONRAD

Photography by

J. STANFIELD PHOTOGRAPHY

Skyhorse Publishing

Dedicated to Flora and Kelly Caldwell

Notice

This book is intended as a reference volume only, not as a medical manual. The information given here is designed to help you make informed decisions about your health. It is not intended as a substitute for any treatment that may have been prescribed by your doctor. If you suspect that you may have medical problems, we urge you to seek competent medical help.

{ Contents }

{ Welcome }

Welcome to *The Paleo Bread Bible*. I wrote, tested, and edited the recipes in this book in my kitchen located in Chattanooga, Tennessee. My mission with *The Paleo Bread Bible* is to create a comprehensive collection of favorite bread recipes and reformulate them to comply as closely as possible with the paleo diet. I abandoned many of the basic tenets that apply to baking with grains and learned how nut flours, palm sugar, coconut milk and oil behave when formulating breads. In many, many instances the recipes are better when converted to paleo versions.

{ Preface }

The paleo diet does not lend itself to easily incorporating bread recipes into the everyday menu. However, I believe the paleo diet approach to health could be very important to the health of many people. For that reason, we should find ways to make it accessible, which means eating bread on occasion. For the most part, the recipes in this book closely adhere to the paleo diet principles. Yes, you will see normally excluded foods (chocolate, coffee, honey, molasses, maple syrup, palm sugar, tapioca flour, alcohol, and more) in some of the recipes because it would be impossible to make some of the recipes without them. Eating paleo breads on an infrequent basis should not set your health goals too far afield. Just make sure you use high quality, organic, whole food and additive-free ingredients whenever possible. For a complete list of foods allowed on the paleo diet see my first cookbook, *The Paleo Diet Cookbook* by Anna Conrad.

{ Stocking Your Pantry }

Stocking your kitchen—Following is a list of standard ingredients you will need to have in your pantry, in addition to typical baking ingredients, before making the recipes in this book. I've listed suppliers for almond flour because almond flour is the main ingredient in many of the recipes, and the suppliers I list here are the best brands to use, based on my experience. I did not list suppliers for other ingredients because I found that the ingredients are widely available from multiple suppliers without much variation in quality.

ALMOND FLOUR AND ALMOND MEAL: Almond flour and almond meal are made by grinding sweet almonds. Almond flour is finely ground blanched almonds. Blanching almonds removes the skin. Almond meal is made with or without the skin on the almonds and it's a less fine grind than almond flour. The consistency of almond meal is similar to that of cornmeal. I used almond flour from 3 suppliers and found them all to be acceptable in the bread recipes. The almond flour suppliers I used are JK Gourmet (www.jkgourmet.com), Benefit Your Life (www.benefityourlifestore.com), and Honeyville (www.honeyvillegrain.com). I ground my own almond meal from whole almonds since I needed smaller quantities.

COCONUT FLOUR: Coconut flour is the meat of a coconut ground finely and defatted. When purchasing, make sure the ingredients state pure coconut flour without any added ingredients like rice flour, sugars, or preservatives. Choose coconut flours that are not pristine white in color because that may indicate unnecessary processing. The color should be similar to coconut flesh, a little off white and creamy colored.

COCONUT OIL: Coconut oil is extracted from the coconut flesh (meat). Coconut oil is used in many paleo recipes and is the primary fat used in this cookbook. Choose virgin coconut oil (VCO) that is made from fresh coconut and mechanically pressed to extract the oil. Other forms of coconut oil can be extracted via chemical or high temperature methods that can reduce the nutrient content and flavor properties of the oil.

COCONUT MILK: Coconut milk is the liquid that comes from squeezing the meat of fresh coconut. Coconut milk can be thick or thin depending on the fat content or whether or not a thickener is added. Canned coconut milk is often diluted with water to achieve a desired fat content. Light coconut milk is the lowest fat containing coconut milk. The recipes in this book are made with canned coconut milk with a 20–22 percent fat content (not light). If possible, choose coconut milk that contains no other ingredients than water. Often thickeners such as guar gum are added and should be avoided if at all possible.

PALM SUGAR: Palm sugar is a nutrient rich, unrefined, low glycemic index, natural sweetener that is obtained by making several slits in the stem of a palm tree, draining liquid, and then boiling until thickened. The boiled product is cooled into cakes and later ground and packaged for sale. Palm sugar is a rich brown color and some say its taste is superior to that of white granulated sugar. Palm sugar behaves much the same as white granulated sugar in baking applications. Palm sugar is not the same as coconut sugar, which is obtained from the cut flowers of the coconut palm tree. The recipes in this book use palm sugar.

BAKING SODA: Baking soda (sodium bicarbonate) is used in baking, as a leavening agent when acidic ingredients are present. Acidic ingredients include phosphates, cream of tartar, lemon juice, yogurt, buttermilk, cacao powder, vinegar, etc. Baking soda reacts with the acidic ingredient and releases carbon dioxide, causing the baked good to rise. Baking soda is often used in combination with baking powder.

BAKING POWDER: Baking powder is a leavening agent composed of a weak acid and a weak base that allows baked goods to rise via an acid-base reaction. Baking powder is used in breads where a fermentation reaction (via yeast) is undesirable because of the taste fermentation imparts. Baked goods or breads that use baking powder to create "lift" of the baked good are often called quick breads because of the quick release of carbon dioxide in the acid-base reaction, yielding shorter processing times (no waiting for bread to rise before baking).

EGGS: Eggs play a critical role in baking by providing protein, fat, and moisture. Protein acts as a binding agent to keep the baked good in one piece vs. crumbly. Fat and moisture provide mouth feel and make the baked good consumable and pleasant to eat vs. dry and hard to chew or swallow. The recipes in this book use more eggs in many of the recipes than a traditional recipe might, especially when coconut flour is incorporated, because the nut flours tend to absorb more moisture than a traditional grain-based flour. Use eggs from free-range chickens or other game birds when possible. The nutrient profile for free-range birds is more paleo friendly than those purchased from mass production farming facilities.

TAPIOCA FLOUR AND ARROWROOT FLOUR: Tapioca flour is derived from cassava root and can be used to make breads as the primary flour component and as a thickening agent to replace cornstarch or grain-based thickeners. Arrowroot flour is often used interchangeably with tapioca flour as a thickener and is acceptable for the paleo diet. I used tapioca flour in the recipes in this book in an attempt to minimize the number of ingredients in my pantry. I also found tapioca flour to be a little less expensive than arrowroot flour. Do not confuse tapioca pearls with tapioca flour for the purpose of the recipes in this book. Purchase the flour form and check the ingredients to make sure it isn't adulterated with wheat flour.

HONEY: Honey is a sweetener created by bees who derive the thick fluid by eating flower nectar and processing it to the point that it dehydrates the sugar and creates natural monosaccharide, fructose, and glucose with a flavor similar in sweetness to granulated white sugar. Because it has a low water content, most harmful microorganisms will not grow in honey. However, honey may contain dormant endospores that are harmful to the immature intestinal tract of infants, which can cause serious illness or even death. For that reason, honey should not be included in recipes that will be eaten by infants. When possible, purchase raw locally produced honey for both environmental reasons and because locally harvested honey will have the flavor of local nectar. Raw honey has a significantly lower glycemic index and a higher nutrient content than commercially produced and packaged honey. If you cannot tolerate raw honey or you will be feeding the baked good to an infant, consider real maple sugar or molasses as a substitute although the flavor profile will vary when using different sugars. Maple syrup is milder and molasses is more robust in flavor.

MAPLE SYRUP: Maple syrup is concentrated syrup obtained from the maple tree. In colder climates, the maple tree stores starch in its trunk and roots before wintertime. The starch is converted to sugar and rises into the sap in the spring. To obtain maple syrup, manufacturers and local artisans bore holes in the tree trunks of maple trees (sugar maple, red maple, and black maple) and boil it to concentrate. Maple syrup has a glycemic index of approximately 54 and it contains manganese, iron, and calcium. Purchase locally produced maple syrup when possible.

MOLASSES: Molasses is a by-product of the manufacturing of granulated sugar or cane sugar. The syrup's flavor, thickness, and nutritional content vary depending upon whether it's the product of the second or third boiling steps during manufacturing. First boiling product in sugar manufacture is "cane syrup" and not molasses. Second boiling is called second molasses and has a slightly bitter flavor. The third boiling produces black strap molasses, which is famous for its robust flavor. Black strap molasses contains calcium, magnesium, potassium, and iron. One tablespoon of black strap molasses is reputed to contain 20 percent of the daily nutritional value for each of these nutrients. Black strap molasses is used in the recipes in this book.

DARK CHOCOLATE (Solid and Powder): Dark chocolate is used in many of the recipes in this book. Choose the darkest organic form available to you. Try to find chocolate that contains 60 percent or greater cacao—70 percent or greater cacao content is ideal. If you find the flavor is too bitter or you aren't getting the melting properties you need, use a little lower cacao content or just give yourself time to adjust to the different flavor profile.

VANILLA EXTRACT: Vanilla extract contains the flavor compound vanillin and is the primary flavor ingredient. Percolating vanilla beans in a solution of ethanol and water creates pure vanilla extract. Purchase "pure" vanilla extract (containing a minimum of 35 percent alcohol and 13.5 ounces per gallon of vanilla beans) for the recipes in this book. Double and triple strength vanilla extract may be available in your area. If you use double or triple strength pure vanilla extract you will need to use only a small fraction of the amount of vanilla listed in the recipes in this book. Do not use imitation vanilla extract as it isn't considered paleo friendly and it's made from by-products derived from the wood pulp industry.

PROBIOTIC CAPSULES: The "sourdough" recipes use probiotics to sour the almond or cashew butter as a starter for the breads and rolls. I purchased probiotic capsules with 10 probiotic strains. I simply used 3–4 capsules for one recipe. Take the capsules apart and empty into the nut butter.

{ Quick Breads }

Banana Bread

Ingredients

1 cup almond flour

1 cup coconut flour

¾ cup palm sugar

¾ teaspoon baking soda

½ teaspoon salt

3 large very ripe bananas, mashed well

6 tablespoons coconut oil, melted and cooled

4 large eggs

¼ cup coconut milk

1 teaspoon vanilla extract

coconut oil to grease the loaf pan

Preparation

1. Adjust an oven rack to the lower-middle position and heat the oven to 350° F. Grease an 8 ½ x 4 ½ inch loaf pan.

2. Whisk the flours, palm sugar, baking soda, and salt together in a large bowl. In a medium bowl, whisk the mashed bananas, coconut oil, eggs, and vanilla together. Gently fold the banana mixture into the flour mixture with a rubber spatula just until combined. The batter will look thick and chunky.

3. Scrape the batter into the prepared pan and smooth the top. Bake until golden brown and a toothpick inserted into the center comes out with just a few crumbs attached, about 55 minutes, rotating the pan halfway through baking.

4. Let the loaf cool in the pan for 10 minutes, then turn out onto a wire rack and let cool for 1 hour before serving.

Chocolate Banana Bread

Ingredients

1 cup almond flour

1 cup coconut flour

10 tablespoons palm sugar

¾ teaspoon baking soda

½ teaspoon salt

3 large very ripe bananas, mashed well

6 tablespoons coconut oil, melted and cooled

2 large eggs

¼ cup coconut milk

1 teaspoon vanilla extract

½ cup grated cacao nibs, chopped coarse

coconut oil for greasing loaf pan

Preparation

1. Adjust an oven rack to the lower-middle position and heat the oven to 350° F. Grease an 8 ½ by 4 ½ inch loaf pan.

2. Whisk the flours, palm sugar, baking soda, cacao nibs, and salt together in a large bowl. In a medium bowl, whisk the mashed bananas, coconut oil, eggs, coconut milk, and vanilla together. Gently fold the banana mixture into the flour mixture with a rubber spatula just until combined. Fold in the walnuts. The batter will look thick and chunky.

3. Scrape the batter into the prepared pan and smooth the top. Bake until golden brown and a toothpick inserted into the center comes out with just a few crumbs attached, about 55 minutes, rotating the pan halfway through baking.

4. Let the loaf cool in the pan for 10 minutes, then turn out onto a wire rack and let cool for 1 hour before serving.

Coconut Banana Bread with Macadamia Nuts

MAKES ONE 8-INCH LOAF

Ingredients

1 cup almond flour

1 cup coconut flour

10 tablespoons palm sugar

¾ teaspoon baking soda

½ teaspoon salt

3 large very ripe bananas, mashed well

6 tablespoons coconut oil, melted and cooled

4 large eggs

¼ cup coconut milk

1 teaspoon vanilla extract

1 cup chopped macadamia nuts, toasted and chopped coarse

½ cup of shredded coconut, toasted

coconut oil to grease the loaf pan

Preparation

1. Adjust an oven rack to the lower-middle position and heat the oven to 350° F. Grease an 8 ½ by 4 ½ inch loaf pan.

2. Whisk the flour, palm sugar, baking soda, and salt together in a large bowl. In a medium bowl, whisk the mashed bananas, coconut oil, eggs, coconut milk, and vanilla together. Gently fold the banana mixture into the flour mixture with a rubber spatula just until combined. Fold in the macadamia nuts and coconut. The batter will look thick and chunky.

3. Scrape the batter into the prepared pan and smooth the top. Bake until golden brown and a toothpick inserted into the center comes out with just a few crumbs attached, about 55 minutes, rotating the pan halfway through baking.

4. Let the loaf cool in the pan for 10 minutes, then turn out onto a wire rack and let cool for 1 hour before serving.

Orange-Spice Banana Bread

Ingredients

1 cup almond flour

1 cup coconut flour

¾ cup palm sugar

¾ teaspoon baking soda

½ teaspoon salt

3 large very ripe bananas, mashed well

6 tablespoons coconut oil, melted and cooled

4 large eggs

¼ cup coconut milk

1 teaspoon vanilla extract

2 tablespoons grated fresh orange zest

1 teaspoon ground cinnamon

¼ teaspoon ground nutmeg

coconut oil for greasing loaf pan

Preparation

1. Adjust an oven rack to the lower-middle position and heat the oven to 350° F. Grease an 8 ½ x 4 ½ inch loaf pan.
2. Whisk the flours, palm sugar, baking soda, orange zest, ground cinnamon, ground nutmeg, and salt together in a large bowl. In a medium bowl, whisk the mashed bananas, coconut oil, eggs, coconut milk, and vanilla together. Gently fold the banana mixture into the flour mixture with a rubber spatula just until combined. The batter will look thick and chunky.
3. Scrape the batter into the prepared pan and smooth the top. Bake until golden brown and a toothpick inserted into the center comes out with just a few crumbs attached, about 55 minutes, rotating the pan halfway through baking.
4. Let the loaf cool in the pan for 10 minutes, then turn out onto a wire rack and let cool for 1 hour before serving.

Zucchini Bread

Ingredients

2 small zucchini, ends trimmed

1 cup almond flour

1 cup coconut flour

1 teaspoon baking soda

1 teaspoon baking powder

1 teaspoon ground cinnamon

1 teaspoon ground allspice

½ teaspoon salt

1 ½ cups palm sugar

6 tablespoons coconut oil, melted
and cooled

2 large eggs

¼ cup coconut milk

1 tablespoon fresh lemon juice

½ cup pecans or walnuts, toasted and
chopped coarse

Preparation

1. Adjust an oven rack to the middle position and heat the oven to 350° F. Grease an 8 ½ x 4 ½ inch loaf pan.

2. Shred the zucchini using the large holes of a box grater. Squeeze the shredded zucchini between several layers of paper towels to absorb excess moisture.

3. Whisk the flours, baking soda, baking powder, cinnamon, allspice, and salt together in a large bowl. In a medium bowl, whisk the palm sugar, coconut oil, eggs, and lemon juice together until smooth. Gently fold the zucchini and yogurt mixture into the flour mixture with a rubber spatula just until combined. Gently fold in pecans or walnuts.

4. Pour the batter into the prepared pan and smooth the top. Bake until golden brown and a toothpick inserted into the center comes out with a few crumbs attached, about 1 hour, rotating the pan halfway through baking.

5. Let the loaf cool in the pan for 10 minutes, then turn onto a wire rack and let cool for 1 hour before serving.

Cranberry-Orange Nut Bread

MAKES ONE 8-INCH LOAF

Ingredients

---

1 ½ cups almond flour

1 ½ cups coconut flour

1 cup palm sugar

1 teaspoon baking powder

½ teaspoon baking soda

½ teaspoon salt

1 ½ cups coconut milk

2 large eggs

8 tablespoons coconut oil, melted and cooled

1 teaspoon grated fresh orange zest

1 ½ cup fresh or frozen cranberries, coarsely chopped

¾ cup toasted walnuts, coarsely chopped

Preparation

1. Adjust an oven rack to the middle position and heat the oven to 350° F. Grease an 8 ½ x 4 ½ inch loaf pan.

2. Whisk the flours, palm sugar, baking powder, baking soda, and salt together in a large bowl. In a medium bowl, whisk the coconut milk and eggs together until smooth. Add the orange zest to the coconut milk mixture. Gently fold the coconut milk mixture into the flour mixture with a rubber spatula just until combined, and then fold in the melted coconut oil. Fold cranberries and walnuts into the batter.

3. Scrape the batter into the prepared pan and smooth the top. Sprinkle almond slices on top of loaf just before baking. Bake until golden brown and a toothpick inserted in the center comes out with just a few crumbs attached, 45 to 55 minutes, rotating the pan halfway through baking.

4. Let the loaf cool in the pan for 10 minutes, then turn out onto a wire rack and let cool for 1 hour before serving.

Date-Nut Bread

Makes One 8-Inch Loaf

Ingredients

2 cups whole dates, chopped coarse

1 cup boiling water

1 teaspoon baking soda

1 cup almond flour

1 cup coconut flour

½ teaspoon salt

1 teaspoon baking powder

¾ cup palm sugar

⅔ cup coconut milk

6 tablespoons coconut oil, melted and cooled

4 large eggs

1 cup pecans or walnuts, toasted and chopped coarse

Preparation

1. Adjust oven rack to the middle position and heat the oven to 350° F. Grease an 8 ½ x 4 ½ inch loaf pan.
2. Stir the dates, water, and baking soda together in a medium bowl. Cover and let sit until the dates have softened, about 30 minutes.
3. Whisk the flours, baking powder, and salt together in a large bowl. In a medium bowl, whisk the palm sugar, coconut milk, and coconut oil together until smooth, then stir in date mixture until combined. Gently fold the coconut milk mixture into the flour mixture with a rubber spatula just until combined. Gently fold in the pecans.
4. Scrape the batter into the prepared pan and smooth the top. Bake until golden brown and a toothpick inserted into the center comes out with just a few crumbs attached, 55 to 60 minutes, rotating the pan halfway through baking.
5. Let the loaf cool in the pan for 10 minutes, then turn out onto a wire rack and let cool for 1 hour before serving.

Spiced Pumpkin Bread

MAKES ONE 8-INCH LOAF

Ingredients

1 cup almond flour

1 cup coconut flour

1 teaspoon baking soda

1 teaspoon baking powder

1 teaspoon ground cinnamon

½ teaspoon salt

½ teaspoon ground nutmeg

½ teaspoon ground ginger

15 ounces canned pumpkin

1 cup palm sugar

8 tablespoons coconut oil, melted
and cooled

4 large eggs

½ cup coconut milk

2 teaspoons vanilla extract

1 cup pecans or walnuts, toasted and
chopped coarse

1 cup dried cranberries

Preparation

1. Adjust an oven rack to the lower-middle position and heat the oven to 350° F. Grease an 8 ½ x 4 ½ inch loaf pan.

2. Whisk the flours, baking soda, baking powder, cinnamon, salt, nutmeg, and ginger together in a large bowl. In a medium bowl, whisk the pumpkin, coconut milk, palm sugar, coconut oil, eggs, and vanilla together until smooth, Gently fold the pumpkin mixture into the flour mixture with a rubber spatula just until combined, do not over mix. Gently fold in the pecans or walnuts and cranberries if using. The batter will be very thick.

3. Scrape the batter into the prepared pan and smooth the top. Bake until golden brown and a toothpick inserted in the center comes out with just a few crumbs attached, 45 to 55 minutes, rotating the pan halfway through baking.

4. Let the loaf cool in the pan for 10 minutes, then turn out onto a wire rack and let cool for 1 hour before serving.

Prune-Nut Bread

MAKES ONE 8-INCH LOAF

Ingredients

---

2 cups whole prunes, chopped coarse

1 cup boiling water

1 teaspoon baking soda

1 cup almond flour

1 cup coconut flour

½ teaspoon salt

1 tablespoon baking powder

¾ cup palm sugar

⅔ cup coconut milk

6 tablespoons coconut oil, melted and cooled

4 large eggs

1 cup pecans or walnuts, toasted and chopped coarse

Preparation

1. Adjust oven rack to the middle position and heat the oven to 350° F. Grease an 8 ½ x 4 ½ inch loaf pan.

2. Stir the prunes, water, and baking soda together in a medium bowl. Cover and let sit until the prunes have softened, about 30 minutes.

3. Whisk the flours, baking powder, and salt together in a large bowl. In a medium bowl, whisk the palm sugar, coconut milk, coconut oil together until smooth, then stir in the prune mixture until combined. Gently fold the coconut milk mixture into the flour mixture with a rubber spatula just until combined. Gently fold in the pecans or walnuts..

4. Scrape the batter into the prepared pan and smooth the top. Bake until golden brown and a toothpick inserted into the center comes out with just a few crumbs attached, 55 to 60 minutes, rotating the pan halfway through baking.

5. Let the loaf cool in the pan for 10 minutes, then turn out onto a wire rack and let cool for 1 hour before serving.

Lemon-Blueberry Bread

MAKES ONE 8-INCH LOAF

Ingredients

1 ½ cups almond flour +1 tablespoon extra

1 ½ cups coconut flour

1 cup palm sugar

1 tablespoon baking powder

½ teaspoon baking soda

½ teaspoon salt

1 ½ cups coconut milk

4 large eggs

8 tablespoons coconut oil, melted and cooled

1 ½ cups fresh or frozen blueberries

1 teaspoon grated fresh lemon zest

Preparation

1. Adjust an oven rack to the middle position and heat the oven to 350° F. Grease an 8 ½ x 4 ½ inch loaf pan.

2. Whisk the flours, palm sugar, baking powder, baking soda, and salt together in a large bowl. In a medium bowl, whisk the coconut milk and eggs together until smooth. Add 1 teaspoon grated fresh lemon zest to the coconut milk mixture. Gently fold the coconut milk mixture into the flour mixture with a rubber spatula just until combined, and then fold in the melted coconut oil. Toss 1 ½ cups fresh or thawed berries with 1 tablespoon flour, and then gently fold into the batter.

3. Scrape the batter into the prepared pan and smooth the top. Bake until golden brown and a toothpick inserted in the center comes out with just a few crumbs attached, 45 to 55 minutes, rotating the pan halfway through baking.

4. Let the loaf cool in the pan for 10 minutes, then turn out onto a wire rack and let cool for 1 hour before serving.

Lemon-Poppy Seed Blueberry Bread

MAKES ONE 8-INCH LOAF

Ingredients

1 ½ cups almond flour +1 tablespoon extra

1 ½ cups coconut flour

1 cup palm sugar

1 tablespoon baking powder

½ teaspoon baking soda

½ teaspoon salt

1 ½ cups coconut milk

4 large eggs

8 tablespoons coconut oil, melted and cooled

1 ½ cups fresh or frozen blueberries

1 teaspoon grated fresh lemon zest

2 tablespoons poppy seeds

Preparation

1. Adjust an oven rack to the middle position and heat the oven to 350° F. Grease an 8 ½ x 4 ½ inch loaf pan.
2. Whisk the flours, palm sugar, baking powder, baking soda, and salt together in a large bowl. In a medium bowl, whisk the coconut milk and eggs together until smooth. Add 1 teaspoon grated fresh lemon zest to the coconut milk mixture. Gently fold the coconut milk mixture into the flour mixture with a rubber spatula just until combined, and then fold in the melted coconut oil. Toss 1 ½ cups fresh or thawed berries with 1 tablespoon flour, then gently fold into the batter.
3. Scrape the batter into the prepared pan and smooth the top. Bake until golden brown and a toothpick inserted in the center comes out with just a few crumbs attached, 45 to 55 minutes, rotating the pan halfway through baking.
4. Let the loaf cool in the pan for 10 minutes, then turn out onto a wire rack and let cool for 1 hour before serving.

Banana-Walnut Bread

MAKES ONE 8-INCH LOAF

Ingredients

1 ½ cups almond flour

1 ½ cups coconut flour

1 cup palm sugar

1 tablespoon baking powder

½ teaspoon baking soda

½ teaspoon salt

½ teaspoon ground nutmeg

1 ½ cups coconut milk

4 large eggs

8 tablespoons coconut oil, melted and cooled

1 ½ cups finely diced bananas

½ cup toasted walnuts, coarsely chopped

coconut oil to grease the loaf pan

Preparation

1. Adjust an oven rack to the middle position and heat the oven to 350° F. Grease an 8 ½ x 4 ½ inch loaf pan.
2. Whisk the flours, palm sugar, baking powder, baking soda, nutmeg, and salt together in a large bowl. In a medium bowl, whisk the coconut milk and eggs together until smooth. Gently fold the coconut milk mixture into the flour mixture with a rubber spatula just until combined, and then fold in the melted coconut oil. Fold the banana pieces and walnuts into the batter.
3. Scrape the batter into the prepared pan and smooth the top. Bake until golden brown and a toothpick inserted in the center comes out with just a few crumbs attached, 45 to 55 minutes, rotating the pan halfway through baking.
4. Let the loaf cool in the pan for 10 minutes, then turn out onto a wire rack and let cool for 1 hour before serving.

Banana-Pecan Bread

MAKES ONE 8-INCH LOAF

Ingredients

2 cups almond flour

1 cup coconut flour

1 cup palm sugar

1 tablespoon baking powder

½ teaspoon baking soda

½ teaspoon salt

½ teaspoon ground nutmeg

1 ½ cups coconut milk

4 large eggs

8 tablespoons coconut oil, melted and cooled

1 ½ cups finely diced bananas

½ cup toasted pecans, coarsely chopped

coconut oil to grease the loaf pan

Preparation

1. Adjust an oven rack to the middle position and heat the oven to 350° F. Grease an 8 ½ x 4 ½ inch loaf pan.

2. Whisk the flours, palm sugar, baking powder, baking soda, nutmeg, and salt together in a large bowl. In a medium bowl, whisk the coconut milk and eggs together until smooth. Gently fold the coconut milk mixture into the flour mixture with a rubber spatula just until combined, and then fold in the melted coconut oil. Fold the banana pieces and pecans into the batter.

3. Scrape the batter into the prepared pan and smooth the top. Bake until golden brown and a toothpick inserted in the center comes out with just a few crumbs attached, 45 to 55 minutes, rotating the pan halfway through baking.

4. Let the loaf cool in the pan for 10 minutes, then turn out onto a wire rack and let cool for 1 hour before serving.

Mocha-Chip Bread

MAKES ONE 8-INCH LOAF

Ingredients

---

1 ½ cups almond flour

1 ½ cups coconut flour

1 cup palm sugar

1 tablespoon baking powder

½ teaspoon baking soda

½ teaspoon salt

3 tablespoons instant espresso

1 ½ cups coconut milk

2 large eggs

8 tablespoons coconut oil, melted and cooled

1 cup cacao nibs

Preparation

1. Adjust an oven rack to the middle position and heat the oven to 350° F. Grease an 8 ½ x 4 ½ inch loaf pan.

2. Whisk the flours, palm sugar, baking powder, baking soda, and salt together in a large bowl. In a medium bowl, whisk the coconut milk and eggs together until smooth. Add the instant espresso to the coconut milk mixture and whisk. Gently fold the coconut milk mixture into the flour mixture with a rubber spatula just until combined, and then fold in the melted coconut oil. Fold the cacao nibs into the batter.

3. Scrape the batter into the prepared pan and smooth the top. Bake until golden brown and a toothpick inserted in the center comes out with just a few crumbs attached, 45 to 55 minutes, rotating the pan halfway through baking.

4. Let the loaf cool in the pan for 10 minutes, then turn out onto a wire rack and let cool for 1 hour before serving.

Apricot-Almond Bread

MAKES ONE 8-INCH LOAF

Ingredients

2 cups almond flour

1 cup coconut flour

1 cup palm sugar

1 tablespoon baking powder

½ teaspoon baking soda

½ teaspoon salt

1 ½ cups coconut milk

4 large eggs

8 tablespoons coconut oil, melted and cooled

½ teaspoon almond extract

1 cup finely diced dried apricots

a few sliced almonds for topping (optional)

Preparation

1. Adjust an oven rack to the middle position and heat the oven to 350° F. Grease an 8 ½ x 4 ½ inch loaf pan.
2. Whisk the flours, sugar, baking powder, baking soda, and salt together in a large bowl. In a medium bowl, whisk the coconut milk and eggs together until smooth. Add the almond extract to the milk mixture. Gently fold the milk mixture into the flour mixture with a rubber spatula just until combined, and then fold in the melted coconut oil. Fold the diced apricots into batter.
3. Scrape the batter into the prepared pan and smooth the top. Sprinkle almond slices on top of loaf just before baking. Bake until golden brown and a toothpick inserted in the center comes out with just a few crumbs attached, 45 to 55 minutes, rotating the pan halfway through baking.
4. Let the loaf cool in the pan for 10 minutes, then turn out onto a wire rack and let cool for 1 hour before serving.

Raspberry-Almond Bread

MAKES ONE 8-INCH LOAF

Ingredients

1 ½ cups almond flour

1 ½ cups coconut flour

1 cup palm sugar

1 tablespoon baking powder

½ teaspoon baking soda

½ teaspoon salt

1 ½ cups coconut milk

4 large eggs

8 tablespoons coconut oil, melted and cooled

½ teaspoon almond extract

¼ cup raspberry jam (See Fruit Jam recipe, page 223)

Preparation

1. Adjust an oven rack to the middle position and heat the oven to 350° F. Grease an 8 ½ x 4 ½ inch loaf pan.

2. Whisk the flours, palm sugar, baking powder, baking soda, and salt together in a large bowl. In a medium bowl, whisk the coconut milk and eggs together until smooth. Add the almond extract to the coconut milk mixture. Gently fold the coconut milk mixture into the flour mixture with a rubber spatula just until combined, and then fold in the melted coconut oil.

3. Scrape ½ of the batter into the prepared pan, and then spoon raspberry jam onto batter. Scrape remaining batter onto raspberry layer and smooth the top. Bake until golden brown and a toothpick inserted in the center comes out with just a few crumbs attached, 45 to 55 minutes, rotating the pan halfway through baking.

4. Let the loaf cool in the pan for 10 minutes, then turn out onto a wire rack and let cool for 1 hour before serving.

Cranberry-Walnut Bread

MAKES ONE 8-INCH LOAF

Ingredients

3 cups almond flour

1 cup palm sugar

1 tablespoon baking powder

½ teaspoon baking soda

½ teaspoon salt

1 ½ cups coconut milk

2 large eggs

8 tablespoons coconut oil, melted and cooled

1 ½ cup fresh or frozen cranberries, coarsely chopped

¾ cup toasted walnuts, coarsely chopped

Preparation

1. Adjust an oven rack to the middle position and heat the oven to 350° F. Grease an 8 ½ x 4 ½ inch loaf pan.

2. Whisk the flour, palm sugar, baking powder, baking soda, and salt together in a large bowl. In a medium bowl, whisk the coconut milk and eggs together until smooth. Gently fold the coconut milk mixture into the flour mixture with a rubber spatula just until combined, and then fold in the melted coconut oil. Fold cranberries and walnuts into the batter.

3. Scrape the batter into the prepared pan and smooth the top. Sprinkle almond slices on top of loaf just before baking. Bake until golden brown and a toothpick inserted in the center comes out with just a few crumbs attached, 45 to 55 minutes, rotating the pan halfway through baking.

4. Let the loaf cool in the pan for 10 minutes, then turn out onto a wire rack and let cool for 1 hour before serving.

Morning Glory Bread

Makes One 8-Inch Loaf

Ingredients

1 ½ cups almond flour

1 ½ cups coconut flour

1 ¼ cups palm sugar

2 teaspoons baking soda

½ teaspoon salt

1 teaspoon ground cinnamon

1 teaspoon vanilla extract

6 large eggs

8 tablespoons coconut oil, melted and cooled

4 medium carrots, peeled and grated

8 ounces fresh pineapple, pressed with paper towels and chopped

½ cup shredded coconut

½ cup raisins

1 cup walnuts or pecans, toasted and chopped coarse

Preparation

1. Adjust an oven rack to the middle position and heat the oven to 350° F. Grease an 8 ½ x 4 ½ inch loaf pan.

2. Whisk the flours, palm sugar, baking soda, cinnamon, and salt together in a large bowl. In a medium bowl, whisk the palm sugar, vanilla, coconut oil and eggs together until smooth. Gently fold the palm sugar mixture into the flour mixture with a rubber spatula just until combined. Fold in the carrots, pineapple, coconut, raisins, and walnuts or pecans just until combined.

3. Scrape the batter into the prepared pan and smooth the top. Bake until golden brown and a toothpick inserted in the center comes out with just a few crumbs attached, 45 to 55 minutes, rotating the pan halfway through baking.

4. Let the loaf cool in the pan for 10 minutes, then turn out onto a wire rack and let cool for 1 hour before serving.

Savory Bacon and Scallion Bread

MAKES ONE 8-INCH LOAF

Ingredients

1 ½ cups almond flour

1 ½ cups coconut flour

1 tablespoon baking powder

1 teaspoon salt

¼ teaspoon cayenne pepper

⅛ teaspoon ground black pepper

4 ounces cooked and crumbled bacon

2 scallions, thinly sliced

1 ¼ cups almond milk

¾ cup coconut milk

1 large egg

3 tablespoons coconut oil, melted and cooled

coconut oil for greasing loaf pan

Preparation

1. Adjust an oven rack to the middle position and heat the oven to 350° F. Grease an 8 ½ x 4 ½ inch loaf pan.

2. Whisk the flours, palm sugar, baking powder, cayenne, pepper, and salt together in a large bowl. Stir in bacon and scallions, breaking up any clumps, until coated with flour. In a medium bowl, whisk the milks, coconut oil, and egg together until smooth. Gently fold the milk mixture into the flour mixture with a rubber spatula just until combined (the batter will be heavy and thick).

3. Scrape the batter into the prepared pan and smooth the top. Bake until golden brown and a toothpick inserted in the center comes out with just a few crumbs attached, 45 to 55 minutes, rotating the pan halfway through baking.

4. Let the loaf cool in the pan for 10 minutes, then turn out onto a wire rack and let cool for 1 hour before serving.

Lemon Tea Bread

MAKES ONE 8-INCH LOAF

Ingredients

1 cup almond flour

¾ cup coconut flour

½ teaspoon baking powder

½ teaspoon salt

6 tablespoons coconut oil, softened

1 ⅓ cups palm sugar

2 tablespoons grated fresh lemon zest

4 large eggs

⅜ cup coconut milk

2 teaspoons fresh lemon juice

coconut oil for greasing loaf pans

Preparation

1. Adjust an oven rack to the middle position and heat the oven to 325° F. Grease and flour an 8 ½ x 4 ½ inch loaf pan.

2. Whisk the flours, baking powder, and salt together in a medium bowl. Whisk the coconut oil, palm sugar, and lemon zest together in a large bowl. Whisk in the eggs until combined, about 30 seconds. Beat in the flour mixture, milk, and lemon juice just until combined.

3. Scrape the batter into the prepared pan and smooth the top. Bake until golden brown and a toothpick inserted into the center comes out with just a few crumbs attached, 45 to 55 minutes, rotating the pan halfway through baking.

4. Let the loaf cool in the pan for 10 minutes, then turn out onto a wire rack and let cool for 1 hour before serving.

Orange Tea Bread

Ingredients

1 cup almond flour

¾ cup coconut flour

½ teaspoon baking powder

½ teaspoon salt

6 tablespoons coconut oil, softened

1 ⅓ cups palm sugar

1 tablespoon grated fresh orange zest

4 large eggs

⅜ cup coconut milk

1 tablespoon fresh orange juice

coconut oil to grease the loaf pan

Preparation

1. Adjust an oven rack to the middle position and heat the oven to 325° F. Grease and flour an 8 ½ x 4 ½ inch loaf pan.

2. Whisk the flours, baking powder, and salt together in a medium bowl. Whisk the coconut oil, palm sugar, and orange zest together in a large bowl. Whisk in the eggs, until combined, about 30 seconds. Whisk in the flour mixture, milk, and orange juice just until combined.

3. Scrape the batter into the prepared pan and smooth the top. Bake until golden brown and a toothpick inserted into the center comes out with just a few crumbs attached, 45 to 55 minutes, rotating the pan halfway through baking.

4. Let the loaf cool in the pan for 10 minutes, then turn out onto a wire rack and let cool for 1 hour before serving.

Almond Tea Bread

Makes One 8-Inch Loaf

Ingredients

1 cup almond flour

¾ cup coconut flour

½ teaspoon baking powder

½ teaspoon salt

6 tablespoons coconut oil, softened

1 ⅓ cups palm sugar

4 large eggs

⅜ cup whole milk

1 teaspoon almond extract

¼ cup almond slices

coconut oil for greasing loaf pan

Preparation

1. Adjust an oven rack to the middle position and heat the oven to 325° F. Grease and flour an 8 ½ x 4 ½ inch loaf pan.

2. Whisk the flours, baking powder, and salt together in a medium bowl. Whisk the coconut oil, palm sugar, and almond extract together in a large bowl. Whisk in the eggs until combined, about 30 seconds. Whisk in the flour mixture and milk just until combined.

3. Scrape the batter into the prepared pan and smooth the top. Top with almond slices. Bake until golden brown and a toothpick inserted into the center comes out with just a few crumbs attached, 45 to 55 minutes, rotating the pan halfway through baking.

4. Let the loaf cool in the pan for 10 minutes, then turn out onto a wire rack and let cool for 1 hour before serving.

Pound Cake Bread

MAKES ONE 8-INCH LOAF

Ingredients

1 cup almond flour

1 cup coconut flour

½ teaspoon baking powder

½ teaspoon salt

½ teaspoon baking soda

8 tablespoons coconut oil, softened

½ cup palm sugar

6 large eggs

1 cup coconut milk

Preparation

1. Adjust an oven rack to the middle position and heat the oven to 325° F. Grease and flour an 8 ½ by 4 ½ inch loaf pan.

2. Whisk the flours, baking powder, salt, and baking soda together in a medium bowl. In a large bowl, whisk the coconut oil and palm sugar together. Whisk in the eggs, one at a time, until combined, about 30 seconds. Whisk in the flour mixture and milk just until combined.

3. Scrape the batter into the prepared pan and smooth the top. Bake until golden brown and a toothpick inserted in the center comes out with just a few crumbs attached, 45 to 55 minutes, rotating the pan halfway through baking.

4. Let the loaf cool in the pan for 10 minutes, then turn out onto a wire rack and let cool for 15 minutes before serving.

Molasses Brown Bread

Makes One 8-Inch Loaf

Ingredients

¾ cup almond meal

1 cup almond flour

1 teaspoon baking soda

½ teaspoon salt

1 cup coconut milk

1 teaspoon lemon juice

⅓ cup dark molasses (do not use blackstrap molasses)

½ cup raisins

1 egg

Preparation

1. Grease an 8 ½ x 4 ½ inch loaf pan. Fold a piece of heavy-duty foil into a 12 x 8 inch rectangle, and grease it on one side. Adjust the oven rack to the middle position and heat the oven to 350° F.
2. Whisk the almond meal, flour, baking soda, and salt together in a large bowl. Stir in the milk, lemon juice, and molasses with a wooden spoon until combined and uniform. Stir in the raisins. Scrape the batter into the prepared pan and smooth the top.
3. Bake until a toothpick inserted in the center comes out with just a few crumbs attached, 45 to 55 minutes, rotating the pan halfway through baking.
4. Let the loaf cool in the pan for 10 minutes, then turn out onto a wire rack and let cool for 1 hour before serving.

The Paleo Bread Bible

Pioneer Bread

Ingredients

1 ¼ cups almond flour

¾ cup almond flour

¼ cup palm sugar

¾ teaspoon baking powder

¾ teaspoon salt

½ teaspoon baking soda

1 cup coconut milk

1 teaspoon lemon juice

¼ cup honey

4 large eggs

½ cup walnuts or pecans, toasted and chopped coarse

¼ cup raisins

¼ cup whole dates, chopped coarse

Preparation

1. Adjust an oven rack to the middle position and heat the oven to 350° F. Grease an 8 ½ x 4 ½ inch loaf pan.
2. Whisk the flours, palm sugar, baking powder, baking soda, and salt together in a large bowl. In a medium bowl, whisk the milk, lemon juice, honey, and eggs together until smooth. Gently fold the egg mixture into the flour mixture with a rubber spatula just until combined. Gently fold in the walnuts or pecans, raisins, and dates.
3. Scrape the batter into the prepared pan and smooth the top. Bake until golden brown and a toothpick inserted into the center comes out with a just a few crumbs attached, about 40 to 45 minutes, rotating the pan halfway through baking.
4. Let the loaf cool in the pan for 10 minutes, then turn out onto a wire back and let cool for 1 hour before serving.

Southern-Style Skillet Almond Meal Bread

SERVES 12

Ingredients

1 ¼ cups almond meal

1 cup almond flour

2 cups coconut milk

1 teaspoon lemon juice

8 tablespoons coconut oil, cut into chunks

1 teaspoon baking powder

1 teaspoon baking soda

¼ teaspoon salt

2 large eggs

Preparation

1. Adjust the oven racks to the lower-middle and middle positions and heat the oven to 450° F. Place a 10-inch cast iron skillet on the middle rack and heat for 10 minutes. Meanwhile, spread the almond meal over a rimmed baking sheet and toast in the oven on the lower-middle rack until fragrant and lightly golden, about 2–4 minutes. Be careful to watch it so it does not burn.

2. Carefully transfer the toasted almond meal to a large bowl and whisk in the almond flour, coconut milk, and lemon juice; set aside. When the skillet is hot, add the coconut oil and return it to the oven, about 5 minutes.

3. Remove the hot skillet from the oven carefully. Pour all but 1 tablespoon of the hot oil into the almond meal mixture, and whisk to incorporate. Then, whisk in the baking powder, baking soda, and salt, followed by the eggs.

4. Quickly scrape the batter into the hot skillet. Bake the almond meal bread until golden brown, 12 to 16 minutes, rotating the bread halfway through baking. Let the bread cool in the skillet for 5 minutes, and then gently flip out onto a wire rack. Serve warm or at room temperature.

Northern Almond Meal Bread

SERVES 6

Ingredients

1 ½ cups almond flour	¾ cup chopped almonds
1 cup almond meal	¼ cup palm sugar
2 teaspoons baking powder	4 large eggs
¾ teaspoon salt	8 tablespoons coconut oil, melted
¼ teaspoon baking soda	and cooled
1 cup coconut milk	coconut oil for greasing pan
1 teaspoon lemon juice	

Preparation

1. Adjust an oven rack to the middle position and heat the oven to 400° F. Grease an 8-inch square baking pan.
2. Whisk the flour, almond meal, baking powder, salt, and baking soda together in a medium bowl until combined.
3. Process the lemon juice, milk, chopped almonds and palm sugar in a food processor until combined, about 5 seconds. Add the eggs and continue to process until well combined, about 5 seconds longer. Pour mixture from processor into a bowl using a spatula to scrape all of the mixture into the bowl.
4. Fold the mixture into the flour mixture with rubber spatula. Fold in the coconut oil just until incorporated.
5. Scrape the batter into the prepared pan and smooth the top. Bake until golden brown and a toothpick inserted into the center comes out with only a few crumbs attached, 25 to 35 minutes, rotating the pan halfway through baking.
6. Let the almond meal bread cool in the pan for 10 minutes, then turn out onto a wire rack and let cool for 20 minutes. Serve warm or at room temperature.

Spicy Jalapeno Almond Meal Bread

SERVES 6

Ingredients

1 ½ cups almond flour

1 cup almond meal

2 teaspoons baking powder

½ teaspoon salt

¼ teaspoon baking soda

1 cup coconut milk

1 teaspoon lemon juice

¼ cup almonds, chopped

2 tablespoons palm sugar

4 large eggs

8 tablespoons coconut oil, melted
    and cooled

1 jalapeno pepper, seeded and minced

¼ teaspoon cayenne

coconut oil for greasing pan

Preparation

1. Adjust an oven rack to the middle position and heat the oven to 400° F. Grease an 8-inch square baking pan.

2. Whisk the flour, almond meal, baking powder, salt, and baking soda together in a medium bowl until combined. Add jalapeno and cayenne pepper to flour mixture.

3. Process the coconut milk, lemon juice, chopped almonds, and palm sugar in a food processor until combined, about 5 seconds. Add the eggs and continue to process until well combined, about 5 seconds longer.

4. Fold the milk mixture into the flour mixture with rubber spatula. Fold in the coconut oil just until incorporated (do not over mix).

5. Scrape the batter into the prepared pan and smooth the top. Bake until golden brown and a toothpick inserted into the center comes out with only a few crumbs attached, 25 to 35 minutes, rotating the pan halfway through baking.

6. Let the almond meal bread cool in the pan for 10 minutes, then turn out onto a wire rack and let cool for 20 minutes. Serve warm or at room temperature.

Blueberry Breakfast Almond Bread

SERVES 6

Ingredients

¾ cup almond flour

¾ cup coconut flour + 1 tablespoon extra

1 cup almond meal

2 teaspoons baking powder

½ teaspoon salt

¼ teaspoon baking soda

¾ cup coconut milk

1 teaspoon lemon juice

¾ cup almonds, chopped

¼ cup palm sugar + 2 tablespoons extra

4 large eggs

8 tablespoons coconut oil, melted
   and cooled

¼ cup maple syrup

1 cup fresh or frozen blueberries
   (do not thaw)

Preparation

1. Adjust an oven rack to the middle position and heat the oven to 400° F. Grease an 8-inch square baking pan.

2. Whisk the flours, almond meal, baking powder, salt, and baking soda together in a medium bowl until combined.

3. Process the coconut milk, lemon juice, maple syrup, chopped almonds, and palm sugar in a food processor until combined, about 5 seconds. Add the eggs and continue to process until well combined, about 5 seconds longer.

4. Fold the coconut milk mixture into the flour mixture with a rubber spatula. Fold in the coconut oil just until incorporated (do not over mix). Toss the blueberries with the 1 tablespoon flour and gently fold into batter.

5. Scrape the batter into the prepared pan and smooth the top. Sprinkle 2 tablespoons palm sugar over loaf before baking. Bake until golden brown and a toothpick inserted into the center comes out with only a few crumbs attached, 25 to 35 minutes, rotating the pan halfway through baking.

6. Let the almond meal bread cool in the pan for 10 minutes, then turn out onto a wire rack and let cool for 20 minutes. Serve warm or at room temperature.

Classic Irish Soda Bread

MAKES ONE 8-INCH ROUND LOAF

Ingredients

3 cups almond flour

1 cup coconut flour

2 tablespoons palm sugar

1 ½ teaspoons baking soda

1 ½ teaspoons cream of tartar

1 ½ teaspoons salt

2 tablespoons coconut oil, softened, for brushing

1 ½ cups coconut milk

1 teaspoon lemon juice

2 tablespoons bacon fat, melted

Preparation

1. Adjust an oven rack to the upper-middle position and heat the oven to 400° F. Line a baking sheet with parchment paper.
2. Whisk the flours, palm sugar, baking soda, cream of tartar, and salt together in a large bowl. Work the oil into the dry ingredients with a fork until the texture resembles coarse crumbs. Stir in the coconut milk and lemon juice with a fork just until the dough begins to come together.
3. Pat the dough into a 6-inch round about 2 inches thick, and lay on the prepared baking sheet.
4. Bake until golden brown and a toothpick inserted into the center comes out with just a few crumbs attached, 40 to 45 minutes, rotating the pan halfway through baking.
5. Let the loaf cool on a wire rack for at least 1 hour. Brush with bacon fat before serving.

American-Style Irish Soda Bread with Raisins and Caraway Seeds

MAKES ONE 8-INCH ROUND LOAF

Ingredients

3 cups almond flour

1 cup coconut flour

¼ cup palm sugar

1 ½ teaspoons baking soda

1 ½ teaspoons cream of tartar

1 ½ teaspoons salt

4 tablespoons coconut oil, softened, plus extra, melted, for brushing

1 ¼ cups coconut milk

1 ⅓ teaspoons lemon juice

2 large eggs

1 cup raisins

1 tablespoon caraway seeds

Preparation

1. Adjust an oven rack to the upper-middle position and heat the oven to 400° F. Line a baking sheet with parchment paper. Whisk the flours, palm sugar, baking soda, cream of tartar, and salt together in a large bowl. Work the coconut oil into the dry ingredients with a fork until the mixture resembles coarse crumbles.

2. Combine coconut milk, lemon juice, and eggs with a fork. Add the milk-egg mixture, raisins, and caraway seeds to flour mixture and stir with a fork just until dough begins to come together. Pat the dough into an 8-inch round about 2 inches thick, and lay on the prepared baking sheet.

3. Bake until golden brown and a toothpick inserted into the center comes out with just a few crumbs attached, 40 to 45 minutes, rotating the pan halfway through baking.

4. Let the loaf cool on a wire rack for at least one hour. Brush with melted oil before serving.

Herb And Scallion Quick Bread

MAKES ONE 8-INCH LOAF

Ingredients

2 ½ cups almond flour

3 tablespoons palm sugar

1 ½ teaspoons baking powder

1 teaspoon baking soda

¾ teaspoon salt

1 cup coconut milk

1 teaspoon lemon juice

8 tablespoons coconut oil, melted and cooled

4 large eggs

5 scallions, sliced thin

1 tablespoon minced fresh thyme

2 tablespoons minced fresh dill

Preparation

1. Adjust an oven rack to the middle position and heat the oven to 350° F. Grease an 8 ½ x 4 ½ inch loaf pan.

2. Whisk the flour, palm sugar, baking powder, baking soda, and salt together in a large bowl. In a medium bowl, whisk the coconut milk, lemon juice, coconut oil, and eggs together until smooth. Gently fold the mixture into the flour mixture with a rubber spatula just until combined (do not over mix). Stir in the scallions, thyme, and dill.

3. Scrape the batter into the prepared loaf pan and smooth the top. Bake until golden brown and a toothpick inserted into the center comes out with just a few crumbs attached, 50 to 55 minutes, rotating the pan halfway through baking.

4. Let the loaf cool in the pan for 10 minutes, then turn out onto a wire rack and let cool for one hour for serving.

Peppercorn and Bacon Bread

MAKES 1 LOAF

Ingredients

2 cups almond flour

½ cup coconut flour

1 teaspoon baking powder

1 teaspoon salt

1 cup almond milk

½ cup coconut milk

2 large eggs

5 slices of bacon, cooked and crumbled

½ cup minced onion

1 teaspoon freshly cracked pepper, black or multicolored

5 tablespoons coconut oil, melted and cooled

Preparation

1. Adjust an oven rack to the middle position and heat the oven to 350° F. Grease an 8 ½ x 4 ½ inch loaf pan.

2. Fry 5 slices of bacon, chopped fine, in a medium skillet over medium heat until crisp, about 8 minutes. Transfer the bacon to paper towe–plate, reserving 3 tablespoons of the fat. Add the reserved fat and a half cup minced onion into the skillet and cook over medium heat until soft, about 3–5 minutes; set aside to cool.

3. Whisk the flours, baking powder, salt, and black pepper together in a large bowl. Stir in the onion and bacon, breaking up clots, until it is coated with the flour mixture. In a medium bowl, whisk the coconut oil and egg together until smooth. Gently fold the milk mixture into the flour mixture with a rubber spatula just until combined. The batter will be heavy and thick.

4. Scrape the batter into the prepared pan and smooth the top. Bake until golden brown and a toothpick inserted into the center comes out with just a few crumbs attached, 45 to 50 minutes, rotating the pan halfway through baking.

5. Let the loaf cool in the pan for 10 minutes, then turn out onto a wire rack and let cool for 1 hour before serving.

{ Muffins }

Big Beautiful Muffins

MAKES 12

Ingredients

2 cups almond flour

1 cup coconut flour

1 cup palm sugar

1 tablespoon baking powder

½ teaspoon salt

1 ½ cups coconut milk

4 large eggs

8 tablespoons coconut oil, melted and cooled

coconut oil for greasing muffin tin

Preparation

1. Adjust an oven rack to the middle position and heat the oven to 375° F. Grease a 12-cup muffin tin.
2. Whisk the flours, palm sugar, baking powder, baking soda, and salt together in a large bowl. In a medium bowl, whisk the coconut milk and eggs together until smooth. Gently fold the milk mixture into the flour mixture with a rubber spatula just until combined, and then fold in the coconut oil.
3. Using a greased ⅓ cup measure, portion the batter into each muffin cup. Bake until golden brown and a toothpick inserted into the center of a muffin comes out with just a few crumbs attached, 25 to 30 minutes, rotating the pan halfway through baking.
4. Let the muffins cool in the pan for 5 minutes, then flip out onto a wire rack and let cool for 10 minutes before serving.

Lemon-Blueberry Muffins

MAKES 12

Ingredients

2 cups almond flour

1 cup coconut flour

1 cup palm sugar

1 tablespoon baking powder

½ teaspoon salt

1 ½ cups coconut milk

4 large eggs

8 tablespoons coconut oil, melted and cooled

1 teaspoon grated fresh lemon zest

1 tablespoon coconut flour

1 ½ cups fresh or frozen blueberries (do not thaw)

coconut oil for greasing muffin tin

Preparation

1. Adjust an oven rack to the middle position and heat the oven to 375° F. Grease a 12-cup muffin tin.

2. Whisk the flours, palm sugar, baking powder, baking soda, and salt together in a large bowl. In a medium bowl, whisk the coconut milk and eggs together until smooth. Add the lemon zest to the coconut milk mixture. Gently fold the coconut milk mixture into the flour mixture with a rubber spatula just until combined, and then fold in the coconut oil. Toss the berries with 1 tablespoon of flour, and then gently fold into the batter.

3. Using a greased ⅓ cup measure, portion the batter into each muffin cup. Bake until golden brown and a toothpick inserted into the center of a muffin comes out with just a few crumbs attached, 25 to 30 minutes, rotating the pan halfway through baking.

4. Let the muffins cool in the pan for 5 minutes, then flip out onto a wire rack and let cool for 10 minutes before serving.

Lemon-Poppy Seed Muffins

MAKES 12

Ingredients

2 cups almond flour

1 cup coconut flour

1 cup palm sugar

1 teaspoon baking powder

½ teaspoon salt

1 ½ cups coconut milk

4 large eggs

8 tablespoons coconut oil, melted
   and cooled

3 tablespoons poppy seeds

1 tablespoon grated lemon zest

¼ cup honey

¼ cup lemon juice

coconut oil for greasing tin

Preparation

1. Adjust an oven rack to the middle position and heat the oven to 375° F. Grease a 12-cup muffin tin.

2. Whisk the flours, palm sugar, baking powder, baking soda, and salt together in a large bowl. In a medium bowl, whisk the coconut milk and eggs together until smooth. Add the lemon zest and poppy seeds to coconut milk mixture. Gently fold the coconut milk mixture into the flour mixture with a rubber spatula just until combined, and then fold in the coconut oil.

3. Using a greased ⅓ cup measure, portion the batter into each muffin cup. Bake until golden brown and a toothpick inserted into the center of a muffin comes out with just a few crumbs attached, 25 to 30 minutes, rotating the pan halfway through baking.

4. While the muffins bake, whisk together the honey and the lemon juice in a small saucepan. Set aside.

5. Let the muffins cool in the pan for 5 minutes, then flip out onto a wire rack and let cool for 10 minutes. Brush the honey syrup over the warm baked muffins before serving.

Banana-Walnut Muffins

Ingredients

2 cups almond flour

1 cup coconut flour

1 cup palm sugar

½ teaspoon ground nutmeg

1 teaspoon baking powder

½ teaspoon salt

1 ½ cups coconut milk

4 large eggs

8 tablespoons coconut oil, melted and cooled

1 ½ cups finely diced banana

½ cup toasted walnuts, coarsely chopped

coconut oil for greasing muffin tin

Preparation

1. Adjust an oven rack to the middle position and heat the oven to 375° F. Grease a 12-cup muffin tin.
2. Whisk the flours, palm sugar, baking powder, baking soda, nutmeg, and salt together in a large bowl. In a medium bowl, whisk the coconut milk and eggs together until smooth. Gently fold the coconut milk mixture into the flour mixture with a rubber spatula just until combined, and then fold in the coconut oil. Gently fold the banana and walnuts into batter.
3. Using a greased ⅓ cup measure, portion the batter into each muffin cup. Bake until golden brown and a toothpick inserted into the center of a muffin comes out with just a few crumbs attached, 25 to 30 minutes, rotating the pan halfway through baking.
4. Let the muffins cool in the pan for 5 minutes, then flip out onto a wire rack and let cool for 10 minutes before serving.

Mocha-Chip Muffins

MAKES 12

Ingredients

2 cups almond flour

1 cup coconut flour

1 cup palm sugar

1 tablespoon baking powder

½ teaspoon salt

3 tablespoons instant espresso

1 cup cacao nibs

1 ½ cups coconut milk

4 large eggs

8 tablespoons coconut oil, melted and cooled

coconut oil for greasing muffin tin

Preparation

1. Adjust an oven rack to the middle position and heat the oven to 375° F. Grease a 12-cup muffin tin.
2. Whisk the flours, palm sugar, baking powder, baking soda, and salt together in a large bowl. In a medium bowl, whisk the coconut milk and eggs together until smooth. Add the espresso to the coconut milk mixture. Gently fold the coconut milk mixture into the flour mixture with a rubber spatula just until combined, and then fold in the coconut oil. Fold the cacao nibs into batter.
3. Using a greased ⅓ cup measure, portion the batter into each muffin cup. Bake until golden brown and a toothpick inserted into the center of a muffin comes out with just a few crumbs attached, 25 to 30 minutes, rotating the pan halfway through baking.
4. Let the muffins cool in the pan for 5 minutes, then flip out onto a wire rack and let cool for 10 minutes before serving.

Apricot-Almond Muffins

MAKES 12

Ingredients

2 cups almond flour

1 cup coconut flour

1 cup palm sugar

1 tablespoon baking powder

½ teaspoon salt

1 ½ cups coconut milk

4 large eggs

8 tablespoons coconut oil, melted and cooled

½ teaspoon almond extract

1 cup finely diced dried apricots

a few sliced almonds for sprinkling on top

coconut oil for greasing muffin tin

Preparation

1. Adjust an oven rack to the middle position and heat the oven to 375° F. Grease a 12-cup muffin tin.

2. Whisk the flours, palm sugar, baking powder, baking soda, and salt together in a large bowl. In a medium bowl, whisk the coconut milk and eggs together until smooth. Add the almond extract to the coconut milk mixture. Gently fold the coconut milk mixture into the flour mixture with a rubber spatula just until combined, and then fold in the coconut oil. Fold in the dried apricot pieces into batter.

3. Using a greased ⅓ cup measure, portion the batter into each muffin cup. Sprinkle tops with sliced almonds before baking. Bake until golden brown and a toothpick inserted into the center of a muffin comes out with just a few crumbs attached, 25 to 30 minutes, rotating the pan halfway through baking.

4. Let the muffins cool in the pan for 5 minutes, then flip out onto a wire rack and let cool for 10 minutes before serving.

Raspberry-Almond Muffins

MAKES 12

Ingredients

---

2 cups almond flour

1 cup coconut flour

1 cup palm sugar

1 tablespoon baking powder

½ teaspoon salt

1 ½ cups coconut milk

4 large eggs

8 tablespoons coconut oil, melted and cooled

½ teaspoon almond extract

¼ cup raspberry jam (see Fruit Jam recipe, page 223)

coconut oil for greasing muffin tin

Preparation

1. Adjust an oven rack to the middle position and heat the oven to 375° F. Grease a 12-cup muffin tin.

2. Whisk the flours, palm sugar, baking powder, baking soda, and salt together in a large bowl. In a medium bowl, whisk the coconut milk and eggs together until smooth. Add the almond extract to the coconut milk mixture. Gently fold the coconut milk mixture into the flour mixture with a rubber spatula just until combined, and then fold in the coconut oil.

3. Using a greased ⅓ cup measure, fill muffin cup halfway, spoon ¼ teaspoon of jam into batter, and then cover the jam with the remaining batter. Bake until golden brown and a toothpick inserted into the center of a muffin comes out with just a few crumbs attached, 25 to 30 minutes, rotating the pan halfway through baking.

4. Let the muffins cool in the pan for 5 minutes, then flip out onto a wire rack and let cool for 10 minutes before serving.

Cranberry-Walnut-Orange Muffins

Ingredients

2 cups almond flour

1 cup coconut flour

1 cup palm sugar

1 tablespoon baking powder

½ teaspoon salt

1 ½ cups coconut milk

4 large eggs

8 tablespoons coconut oil, melted and cooled

1 teaspoon grated orange zest

1 ½ cups fresh or frozen cranberries

¾ cup toasted walnuts, coarsely chopped

coconut oil for greasing muffin tin

Preparation

1. Adjust an oven rack to the middle position and heat the oven to 375° F. Grease a 12-cup muffin tin.

2. Whisk the flours, palm sugar, baking powder, baking soda, and salt together in a large bowl. In a medium bowl, whisk the coconut milk and eggs together until smooth. Add the orange zest to the coconut milk mixture. Gently fold the coconut milk mixture into the flour mixture with a rubber spatula just until combined, and then fold in the coconut oil. Add the cranberries and walnuts into the batter and mix until combined.

3. Using a greased ⅓ cup measure, portion the batter into each muffin cup. Bake until golden brown and a toothpick inserted into the center of a muffin comes out with just a few crumbs attached, 25 to 30 minutes, rotating the pan halfway through baking.

4. Let the muffins cool in the pan for 5 minutes, then flip out onto a wire rack and let cool for 10 minutes before serving.

Almond-Meal Raisin Muffins

MAKES 12

Ingredients

1 cup raisins

1 teaspoon water

2 ½ cups almond meal

⅔ cup palm sugar

3 tablespoons molasses

3 large eggs

1 teaspoon vanilla extract

6 tablespoons coconut oil, melted
   and cooled

1 ¾ cups coconut milk

2 ¾ cups almond flour

2 teaspoons baking soda

½ teaspoon salt

coconut oil for greasing tin

Preparation

1. Adjust an oven rack to the middle position and heat the oven to 400° F. Grease a 12-cup muffin tin.

2. Combine the raisins and water in a small microwave-safe bowl, and cover tightly with plastic wrap. Poke several small steam vents in the plastic wrap and microwave on high power for 30 seconds. Let stand, covered, until the raisins are softened and plump, about 5 minutes. Transfer the raisins to a paper towel-lined plate; set aside to cool.

3. In a medium bowl whisk the palm sugar, molasses, whole egg, egg yolk, and vanilla together until the mixture is thick in uniform. Whisk the coconut oil, coconut milk, and almond meal to combine.

4. In a large bowl, whisk the flours, baking soda, and salt together. Gently fold the almond meal mixture into the flour mixture with a rubber spatula just until combined (do not over mix). Fold in the cooled raisins.

5. Using a greased ⅓ cup measure, portion the batter into each muffin cup. Bake the muffins until dark golden and a toothpick inserted in the center comes out with only a few crumbs attached, about 15 to 20 minutes, rotating the pan halfway through baking.

6. Let the muffins cool in the pan for 5 minutes, and then flip out onto a wire rack and let cool for 10 minutes before serving.

Coffee Cake Muffins

MAKES 12

Ingredients

1 cup palm sugar

1 cup almond flour

½ cup coconut flour

½ cup palm sugar

1 tablespoon ground cinnamon

½ teaspoon baking powder

½ teaspoon salt

¼ teaspoon baking soda

12 tablespoons coconut oil, cut into 1 inch
    pieces and chilled

6 large eggs

½ cup coconut milk

coconut oil for greasing muffin tin

Preparation

1. Adjust an oven rack to the middle position and heat the oven to 350° F. Grease a 12-cup muffin tin.

2. Pulse the palm sugar and coconut flour together in a food processor to combine, about 5 pulses. Transfer ¾ cup of the processed palm sugar mixture to a medium bowl (leaving the rest in the processor). Whisk in the ¼ cup palm sugar and cinnamon to make the streusel; set aside.

3. Add the almond flour, the baking powder, salt, and baking soda to the palm sugar mixture left in the food processor and pulse to combine, about 5 pulses. Scatter the coconut oil pieces evenly over the top, and pulse until the mixture breaks down into small pebbly pieces, about 10 pulses. Add the eggs and coconut milk and pulse until the batter is well combined and thick, about 8 pulses.

4. Portion a generous tablespoon of the batter into each muffin cup, and then sprinkle each with 1 ½ tablespoons of the streusel mixture. Spoon the remaining batter over the streusel. Bake until golden brown and a toothpick inserted into the center of the muffin comes out with just a few crumbs attached, 20 to 25 minutes, rotating the pan halfway through baking.

5. Let the muffins cool in the pan for 5 minutes, then flip out onto a wire rack and let cool for 10 minutes.

Coffee Cake Muffins with Honey Glaze

MAKES 12

Ingredients

1 cup palm sugar	¼ teaspoon baking soda
1 cup almond flour	12 tablespoons coconut oil, cut into 1-inch
½ cup coconut flour	pieces and chilled
½ cup palm sugar	6 large eggs
1 tablespoon ground cinnamon	½ cup coconut milk
½ teaspoon baking powder	¼ cup honey
½ teaspoon salt	coconut oil for greasing muffin tin

Preparation

1. Adjust an oven rack to the middle position and heat the oven to 350° F. Grease a 12-cup muffin tin.

2. Pulse the palm sugar and coconut flour together in a food processor to combine, about 5 pulses. Transfer ¾ cup of the processed palm sugar mixture to a medium bowl (leaving the rest in the processor). Whisk in the remaining ¼ cup palm sugar and cinnamon to make the streusel topping; set aside.

3. Add the almond flour, the baking powder, salt, and baking soda to the palm sugar mixture left in the food processor and pulse to combine, about 5 pulses. Scatter the coconut oil pieces evenly over the top, and pulse until the mixture breaks down into small pebbly pieces, about 10 pulses. Add the eggs and coconut milk and pulse until the batter is well combined and thick, about 8 pulses.

4. Portion a generous tablespoon of the batter into each muffin cup, and then sprinkle each with 1 ½ tablespoons of the streusel mixture. Spoon the remaining batter over the streusel. Bake until golden brown and a toothpick inserted into the center of the muffin comes out with just a few crumbs attached, 20 to 25 minutes, rotating the pan halfway through baking.

5. Let the muffins cool in the pan for 5 minutes, then flip out onto a wire rack and let cool for 10 minutes. Place a sheet of parchment paper under a wire rack as the muffins cool.

6. Spoon about 2 teaspoons of the honey over each of the muffins, letting it run down the sides.

Coffee Cake Muffins with Cacao Nibs

MAKES 12

Ingredients

1 cup palm sugar

1 cup almond flour

½ cup coconut flour

½ cup palm sugar

1 tablespoon ground cinnamon

½ teaspoon baking powder

½ teaspoon salt

¼ teaspoon baking soda

12 tablespoons coconut oil, cut into 1-inch pieces and chilled

6 large eggs

½ cup coconut milk

½ cup cacao nibs

coconut oil for greasing muffin tin

Preparation

1. Adjust an oven rack to the middle position and heat the oven to 350° F. Grease a 12-cup muffin tin.
2. Pulse the palm sugar and coconut flour together in a food processor to combine, about 5 pulses. Transfer ¾ cup of the processed palm sugar mixture to a medium bowl (leaving the rest in the processor). Whisk in the remaining ¼ cup palm sugar and cinnamon to make the streusel; set aside.
3. Add the almond flour, the baking powder, salt, and baking soda to the palm sugar mixture left in the food processor and pulse to combine, about 5 pulses. Scatter the coconut oil pieces evenly over the top, and pulse until the mixture breaks down into small pebbly pieces, about 10 pulses. Add the eggs and coconut milk and pulse until the batter is well combined and thick, about 8 pulses.
4. Portion a generous tablespoon of the batter into each muffin cup, sprinkle each with 1 ½ tablespoons of the streusel mixture, and then 10 cacao nibs. Spoon the remaining batter over the streusel and cacao nibs. Bake until golden brown and a toothpick inserted into the center of the muffin comes out with just a few crumbs attached, 20 to 25 minutes, rotating the pan halfway through baking.
5. Let the muffins cool in the pan for 5 minutes, then flip out onto a wire rack and let cool for 10 minutes.

Coffee Cake Muffins with Toasted Nuts

Ingredients

1 cup palm sugar

1 cup almond flour

½ cup coconut flour

1/2 cup palm sugar

1 tablespoon ground cinnamon

½ teaspoon baking powder

½ teaspoon salt

¼ teaspoon baking soda

12 tablespoons coconut oil, cut into 1-inch pieces and chilled

6 large eggs

½ cup coconut milk

¼ cup nuts (walnuts, almonds or pecans) toasted and coarsely chopped

coconut oil for greasing muffin tin

Preparation

1. Adjust an oven rack to the middle position and heat the oven to 350° F. Grease a 12-cup muffin tin.

2. Pulse the 1 cup palm sugar and the coconut flour together in a food processor to combine, about 5 pulses. Transfer ¾ cup of the processed palm sugar mixture to a medium bowl (leaving the rest in the processor). Whisk in the ¼ cup palm sugar and cinnamon to make the streusel; set aside.

3. Add the almond flour, the baking powder, salt, and baking soda to the palm sugar mixture left in the food processor and pulse to combine, about 5 pulses. Scatter the coconut oil pieces evenly over the top, and pulse until the mixture breaks down into small pebbly pieces, about 10 pulses. Add the eggs and coconut milk and pulse until the batter is well combined and thick, about 8 pulses.

4. Portion a generous tablespoon of the batter into each muffin cup, and then sprinkle each with 1 ½ tablespoons of the streusel mixture and 1 teaspoon of toasted nuts. Spoon the remaining batter over the streusel and nut layers. Bake until golden brown and a toothpick inserted into the center of the muffin comes out with just a few crumbs attached, 20 to 25 minutes, rotating the pan halfway through baking.

5. Let the muffins cool in the pan for 5 minutes, then flip out onto a wire rack and let cool for 10 minutes.

Morning Glory Muffins

MAKES 12

Ingredients

1 ¾ cups almond flour

½ cup coconut flour

2 teaspoons baking soda

1 teaspoon ground cinnamon

½ teaspoon salt

1 ¼ cups palm sugar

6 large eggs

8 tablespoons coconut oil, melted and
  cooled

1 teaspoon vanilla extract

4 medium carrots, peeled and grated

8 ounces fresh pineapple, pressed dry with
  paper towels

½ cup shredded coconut

½ cup raisins

1 cup walnuts or pecans, toasted and
  chopped coarse

coconut oil to grease muffin tin

Preparation

1. Adjust an oven rack to the middle position and heat the oven to 375° F. Grease a 12-cup muffin tin.

2. Whisk the flours, baking soda, cinnamon, and salt together in a large bowl. In a small bowl, whisk the palm sugar, eggs, coconut oil, and vanilla together until smooth. Gently fold the palm sugar mixture into the flour mixture with a rubber spatula just until combined. Fold in the carrots, pineapple, coconut, raisins, and walnuts or pecans just until combined.

3. Using a greased ⅓ cup measure, portion the batter into each muffin cup. Bake until golden brown and a toothpick inserted in the center of a muffin comes out with just a few crumbs attached, 25 to 30 minutes, rotating the pan halfway through baking.

4. Let the muffins cool in the pan for 5 minutes, then flip out onto a wire rack and let cool for 10 minutes before serving.

Apricot Muffins with Orange Essence

MAKES 12

Ingredients

Orange Palm Sugar

⅔ cup palm sugar

1 ½ teaspoons grated fresh orange zest

Batter

1 ½ cups dried apricots, chopped fine

½ cup orange juice

1 ½ cups almond flour

½ cup coconut flour

1 cup almond meal

1 ½ teaspoons baking powder

1 teaspoon baking soda

1 teaspoon salt

1 ¼ cups coconut milk

¾ cup palm sugar

8 tablespoons coconut oil,
    melted and cooled

4 large eggs

½ teaspoon grated fresh orange zest

coconut oil for greasing muffin tin

Preparation

1. FOR THE ORANGE PALM SUGAR: Process the palm sugar and orange zest in a food processor for about 10 seconds; set aside.
2. FOR THE BATTER: Adjust an oven rack to the middle position and heat the oven to 400° F. Grease a 12-cup muffin tin.
3. Combine apricots and orange juice in a medium microwave-safe bowl and cover tightly with plastic wrap. Poke several small steam vents in the plastic wrap and microwave on high power until simmering, about 1 minute. Let stand, covered, until the apricots are softened and plumped, about 5 minutes. Transfer the apricots to a paper towel-lined plate; set aside to cool.
4. Whisk the flours, almond meal, baking powder, baking soda, and salt together in a large bowl. In a medium bowl, whisk the coconut milk, palm sugar, coconut oil, eggs, and orange zest together until smooth, then stir in the cooled apricots. Gently fold the coconut milk mixture into the flour mixture with a rubber spatula until combined.
5. Using a greased ⅓ cup measure, portion the batter into each muffin cup. Sprinkle the orange palm sugar over the tops of the muffins. Bake until golden brown and a toothpick inserted in the center of a muffin comes out with just a few crumbs attached, 15 to 20 minutes, rotating the pan halfway through baking.

Savory Bacon and Scallion Muffins

MAKES 12

Ingredients

2 cups almond flour

1 cup coconut flour

1 tablespoon baking powder

1 teaspoon salt

¼ teaspoon cayenne pepper

⅛ teaspoon ground black pepper

5 slices bacon, cooked and crumbled

2 scallions, thinly sliced

2 cups coconut milk

3 tablespoons coconut oil, melted and cooled

2 large eggs

coconut oil for greasing muffin tin

Preparation

1. Adjust an oven rack to the middle position and heat the oven to 350° F. Grease a 12-cup muffin tin.

2. Whisk the flours, baking powder, salt, cayenne, and pepper together in a large bowl. Stir in the bacon and scallions, breaking up any clots, until the bacon is coated with flour. In a medium bowl whisk the coconut milk, coconut oil, and eggs together until smooth. Gently fold the coconut milk mixture into the flour mixture with a rubber spatula just until combined (the batter will be heavy and thick).

3. Using a greased ⅓ cup measure, portion the batter into each muffin cup. Bake until golden brown and a toothpick inserted in the center of a muffin comes out with just a few crumbs attached, 25 to 30 minutes, rotating the pan halfway through baking.

4. Let the muffins cool in the pan for 5 minutes, then flip out onto a wire rack and let cool for 10 minutes before serving.

{ Scones and Biscuits }

Simple Drop Biscuits

MAKES 12

Ingredients

1 cup almond flour

1 cup coconut flour

2 teaspoons baking powder

½ teaspoon baking soda

1 teaspoon palm sugar

¾ teaspoon salt

1 cup coconut milk, chilled

8 tablespoons coconut oil, melted and slightly cooled, plus extra for brushing

Preparation

1. Adjust an oven rack to the middle position and heat the oven to 475° F. Line a baking sheet with parchment paper.

2. Whisk the flours, baking powder, baking soda, palm sugar, and salt together in a large bowl. In a medium bowl, stir the chilled coconut milk and melted coconut oil together until small clumps form. Stir the coconut milk mixture into the flour mixture with a rubber spatula just until incorporated and the dough pulls away from the sides of the bowl.

3. Using greased hands, shape dough into round biscuit shapes and place the mounds onto the prepared baking sheet, spacing them about 1 ½ inches apart. Bake until the tops are golden brown and crisp, 12 to 14 minutes, rotating the pan halfway through baking.

4. Brush the baked biscuits with extra melted coconut oil, transfer to a wire rack, and let cool for 5 minutes. Serve warm.

Sour Biscuits

MAKES 12

Ingredients

3 cups almond flour

¾ cup coconut flour + extra for rolling

½ cup powdered coconut milk

2 tablespoons palm sugar

4 teaspoons baking powder

1 ½ teaspoons salt

1 teaspoon baking soda

12 tablespoons coconut oil, cut into ½-inch pieces and chilled

1 ¼ cups coconut milk

2 teaspoons lemon juice

Preparation

1. Adjust an oven rack to the middle position and heat the oven to 450° F. Line a baking sheet with parchment paper.

2. Pulse the flours, coconut milk powder, lemon juice, palm sugar, baking powder, salt, and baking soda together in a food processor to combine, about 3 pulses. Scatter the coconut oil and shortening evenly over the top, and continue to pulse until the mixture resembles coarse meal, about 15 pulses.

3. Transfer the flour mixture to a large bowl. Stir in the milk with a rubber spatula until the dough comes together.

4. Using your hands, shape 12 portions into 2 ½ inch round and 1 inch thick biscuits. Arrange the biscuits on the prepared baking sheet, space about 1 ½ inches apart.

5. Bake for 5 minutes. Rotate the pan, reduce the oven temperature to 400° F, and continue to bake until golden brown, 12-15 minutes. Transfer to a wire rack, let cool for 5 minutes, and serve warm.

To Make Ahead

Unbaked biscuits can be covered and refrigerated for up to 24 hours; bake as directed. (They do not freeze well.)

Coconut Cream Biscuits

MAKES 8

Ingredients

1 ½ cups almond flour

½ cup coconut flour + extra for rolling

2 teaspoons palm sugar

2 teaspoons baking powder

½ teaspoon salt

1 ½ cups coconut milk

Preparation

1. Adjust an oven rack to the upper middle position and heat the oven to 450° F. Line a baking sheet with parchment paper.
2. Whisk the flours, palm sugar, baking powder, and salt together in a large bowl. Stir in the coconut milk with a wooden spoon until the dough forms.
3. Using your hands, shape 8 portions of dough into 2 ½ inch round and ¾ inch thick biscuits. Arrange the biscuits onto the prepared baking sheet, space about 1 ½ inches apart.
4. Bake the biscuits until lightly browned, 15 to 17 minutes, rotating the pan halfway through baking.
5. Remove from oven and transfer to a wire rack, let cool for 5 minutes, and serve warm.

Double It

To double the coconut cream biscuit recipe, double all of the ingredients, and prepare the biscuits as directed. Arrange the biscuits onto prepared baking sheets and bake as directed, one tray at a time.

To Make Ahead

Unbaked biscuits can be covered and refrigerated for up to 2 hours; bake as directed. They can also be frozen for up to one month; cover and freeze the biscuits until frozen solid, about 6 hours, then transfer to a large zipper lock bag. Bake the frozen biscuits (do not thaw) as directed, increasing the baking time to 20 to 25 minutes.

Sweet Potato Biscuits

MAKES 8

Ingredients

1 large sweet potato, peeled and cut into ½-inch cubes	2 tablespoons palm sugar
1 ½ cups coconut milk	1 teaspoon baking powder
¼ teaspoon vanilla extract	1 teaspoon salt
2 cups almond flour	½ teaspoon baking soda
½ cup coconut flour	¼ teaspoon ground cinnamon
	1 pinch ground nutmeg

Preparation

1. Adjust an oven rack to the upper-middle position and heat the oven to 400° F. Line a baking sheet with parchment paper.
2. Place the cubed sweet potato in a medium microwave-safe bowl and cover tightly with plastic wrap. Poke 2 small steam vents in the plastic and microwave on high power until the potatoes are tender, 5 to 7 minutes. Mash the cooked potatoes with a potato masher until very smooth and let cool slightly.
3. Whisk the coconut milk and vanilla into the mashed sweet potato until thoroughly combined. In a large bowl, whisk the flours, palm sugar, baking powder, salt, baking soda, cinnamon, and nutmeg together. Stir the sweet potato mixture into the flour mixture with a wooden spoon until the dough forms, about 30 seconds. It will be wet and sticky.
4. Spoon ¼ cup of dough out onto a prepared cookie sheet about 1 ½ inches apart; repeat for the remaining dough.
5. Bake until the biscuits are lightly browned, 9 to 11 minutes, rotating the pan halfway through baking.
6. Remove from oven and transfer to a wire rack, let cool for 5 minutes, and serve warm.

To Make Ahead

Unbaked biscuits can be covered and refrigerated for up to 2 hours; bake as directed. They can also be frozen for up to one month; cover and freeze the biscuits until frozen solid, about 6 hours, then transfer to a large zipper lock bag. Bake the frozen biscuits (do not thaw) as directed, increasing the baking time to 20 to 25 minutes.

Simple Coconut Cream Scones

MAKES 8

Ingredients

1 ½ cups almond flour

½ cup coconut flour

3 tablespoons palm sugar

1 tablespoon baking powder

½ teaspoon salt

5 tablespoons coconut oil, cut into ¼-inch pieces and chilled

½ cup currants (optional)

1 cup coconut milk

coconut oil for greasing a 9-inch square baking dish

Preparation

1. Adjust an oven rack to the middle position and heat the oven to 450° F. Line the 9-inch baking dish with parchment paper.
2. Pulse the flours, palm sugar, baking powder, and salt together in a food processor to combine, about 3 pulses. Scatter the coconut oil evenly over the top and continue to pulse until the mixture resembles coarse cornmeal with a few slightly larger coconut oil lumps, about 12 more pulses. Transfer the mixture to a large bowl and stir in the currants (if using). Stir in the coconut milk with a rubber spatula until the dough begins to form, about 30 seconds.
3. Press the dough into the prepared 9-inch baking dish. Unmold the dough and cut into 8 wedges.
4. Place the wedges on the prepared baking sheet. Bake until the scone tops are lightly golden brown, 12 to 15 minutes, rotating the pan halfway through baking. Transfer to a wire rack, and let cool for at least 10 minutes. Serve warm or at room temperature.

Simple Ginger Cream Scones

MAKES 8

Ingredients

1 ½ cups almond flour

½ cup coconut flour

3 tablespoons sugar

1 tablespoon baking powder

½ teaspoon salt

5 tablespoons unsalted butter, cut into ¼-inch pieces and chilled

½ cup grated ginger or 1 teaspoon ginger powder

1 cup coconut milk

coconut oil for greasing a 9-inch baking dish

Preparation

1. Adjust an oven rack to the middle position and heat the oven to 450° F. Line the 9-inch baking dish with parchment paper.

2. Pulse the flours, sugar, baking powder, ginger, and salt together in a food processor to combine, about 3 pulses. Scatter the butter evenly over the top and continue to pulse until the mixture resembles coarse cornmeal with a few slightly larger butter lumps, about 12 more pulses. Transfer the mixture to a large bowl and stir in the ginger. Stir in the coconut milk with a rubber spatula until the dough begins to form, about 30 seconds.

3. Turn the dough and any floury bits out onto a floured counter and knead until it forms a rough, slightly sticky ball. Press the dough into the greased 9-inch baking dish. Unmold the dough and cut into 8 wedges.

4. Place the wedges on the prepared baking sheet. Bake until the scone tops are lightly golden brown, 12 to 15 minutes, rotating the pan halfway through baking. Transfer to a wire rack, and let cool for at least 10 minutes. Serve warm or at room temperature.

Simple Cranberry-Orange Cream Scones

MAKES 8

Ingredients

1 ½ cups almond flour

½ cup coconut flour

3 tablespoons sugar

1 tablespoon baking powder

½ teaspoon salt

5 tablespoons unsalted butter, cut into ¼-inch pieces and chilled

¾ cup dried cranberries

1 teaspoon grated fresh orange zest

1 cup coconut milk

coconut oil for greasing a 9-inch baking dish

Preparation

1. Adjust an oven rack to the middle position and heat the oven to 450° F. Line a baking dish with parchment paper.

2. Pulse the flours, sugar, baking powder, and salt together in a food processor to combine, about 3 pulses. Scatter the butter and orange zest evenly over the top and continue to pulse until the mixture resembles coarse cornmeal with a few slightly larger butter lumps, about 12 more pulses. Transfer the mixture to a large bowl and stir in the cranberries. Stir in the coconut milk with a rubber spatula until the dough begins to form, about 30 seconds. Press the dough into the greased 9-inch baking dish. Unmold the dough and cut into 8 wedges.

3. Place the wedges on the prepared baking sheet. Bake until the scone tops are lightly golden brown, 12 to 15 minutes, rotating the pan halfway through baking. Transfer to a wire rack, and let cool for at least 10 minutes. Serve warm or at room temperature.

Almond Meal Scones

MAKES 8

Ingredients

1 ½ cups almond meal

¼ cup coconut milk

1 large egg

½ cup almond flour

⅓ cup palm sugar, plus extra for sprinkling

2 teaspoons baking powder

½ teaspoon salt

10 tablespoons coconut oil, cut into ¼-inch
    pieces and chilled

Preparation

1. Adjust an oven rack to the middle position and heat the oven to 375° F. Spread the almond meal out onto a rimmed baking sheet and toast in the oven until lightly browned, about 8 minutes, shaking the pan occasionally. Let cool on a wire rack; when the almond meal is cooled, measure out 2 tablespoons and reserve for dusting.

2. Increase the oven temperature to 450° F. Line a baking sheet with parchment paper. Whisk the milk, and egg together in a large measuring cup. Measure out 1 tablespoon of the mixture and reserve for glazing.

3. Pulse the flour, palm sugar, baking powder, and salt together in a food processor to combine, about 3 pulses. Scatter the coconut oil evenly over the top and continue to pulse until the mixture resembles coarse cornmeal, 12 to 14 pulses. Transfer the mixture to a medium bowl and stir in the cooled almond meal. Fold in the milk mixture with a rubber spatula until the dough begins to form, about 30 seconds.

4. Dust the counter with half of the reserved almond meal. Turn the dough out onto the counter and dust the top with the remaining almond meal. Pat the dough into a 7-inch round, about 1 inch thick. Cut the dough into 8 wedges.

5. Place the wedges on the prepared baking sheet, brush with the reserved milk mixture, and sprinkle lightly with palm sugar. Bake until the scone tops are golden, 12 to 15 minutes, rotating the pan halfway through baking. Transfer to a wire rack and let cool for at least 10 minutes. Serve warm or at room temperature.

Cinnamon-Raisin Almond Meal Scones

MAKES 8

Ingredients

1 ½ cups almond meal

½ cup coconut milk

2 large eggs

½ cups almond flour

½ teaspoon cinnamon

⅓ cup palm sugar, plus extra for sprinkling

2 teaspoons baking powder

½ teaspoon salt

10 tablespoons coconut oil, cut into ¼ inch pieces and chilled

1 cup golden raisins

Preparation

1. Adjust an oven rack to the middle position and heat the oven to 375° F. Spread the almond meal out onto a rimmed baking sheet and toast in the oven until lightly browned, about 8 minutes, shaking the pan occasionally. Let cool on a wire rack; when the almond meal is cooled, measure out 2 tablespoons and reserve for dusting.

2. Increase the oven temperature to 450° F. Line a baking sheet with parchment paper. Whisk the milk, and eggs together in a large measuring cup. Measure out 1 tablespoon of the mixture and reserve for glazing.

3. Pulse the flour, palm sugar, baking powder, cinnamon, and salt together in a food processor to combine, about 3 pulses. Scatter the coconut oil evenly over the top and continue to pulse until the mixture resembles coarse cornmeal, 12 to 14 pulses. Transfer the mixture to a medium bowl and stir in the almond meal and raisins. Fold in the milk mixture with a rubber spatula until the dough begins to form, about 30 seconds.

4. Dust the counter with half of the reserved almond meal. Turn the dough out onto the counter and dust the top with the remaining almond meal. Pat the dough into a greased 7-inch round, about 1 inch thick. Unmold the dough and cut the dough into 8 wedges.

5. Place the wedges on the prepared baking sheet, brush with the reserved milk / egg mixture, and sprinkle lightly with palm sugar. Bake until the scone tops are golden, 12 to 15 minutes, rotating the pan halfway through baking. Transfer to a wire rack and let cool for at least 10 minutes. Serve warm or at room temperature.

Glazed Maple-Pecan Almond Meal Scones

Makes 8

Ingredients

1 ½ cups almond meal

½ cup coconut milk

2 large eggs

⅜ cup almond flour

⅛ cup coconut flour

¼ cup maple syrup + 3 tablespoons extra

½ cup palm sugar

2 teaspoons baking powder

½ teaspoon salt

10 tablespoons coconut oil, cut into ¼-inch pieces and chilled

1 cup pecans coarsely chopped

Preparation

1. Adjust an oven rack to the middle position and heat the oven to 375° F. Spread the almond meal out onto a rimmed baking sheet and toast in the oven until lightly browned, about 8 minutes, shaking the pan occasionally. Let cool on a wire rack; when the almond meal is cooled, measure out 2 tablespoons and reserve for dusting.

2. Increase the oven temperature to 450° F. Line a baking sheet with parchment paper. Whisk the milk, ¼ cup maple syrup and eggs together in a large measuring cup. Measure out 1 tablespoon of the mixture and reserve for glazing.

3. Pulse the flour, palm sugar, baking powder, and salt together in a food processor to combine, about 3 pulses. Scatter the coconut oil evenly over the top and continue to pulse until the mixture resembles coarse cornmeal, 12 to 14 pulses. Transfer the mixture to a medium bowl and stir in the cooled almond meal. Fold in the milk mixture with a rubber spatula until the dough begins to form, about 30 seconds.

4. Dust the counter with half of the reserved almond meal. Turn the dough out onto the counter and dust the top with the remaining almond meal. Pat the dough into a greased 7-inch round, about 1 inch thick. Cut the dough into 8 wedges.

5. Place the wedges on the prepared baking sheet, brush with the reserved milk mixture, and sprinkle lightly with palm sugar. Bake until the scone tops are golden, 12 to 15 minutes, rotating the pan halfway through baking. Transfer to a wire rack and let cool for at least 10 minutes.

6. After scones have cooled, whip 3 tablespoons maple syrup to form a glaze. Drizzle the glaze over the scones.

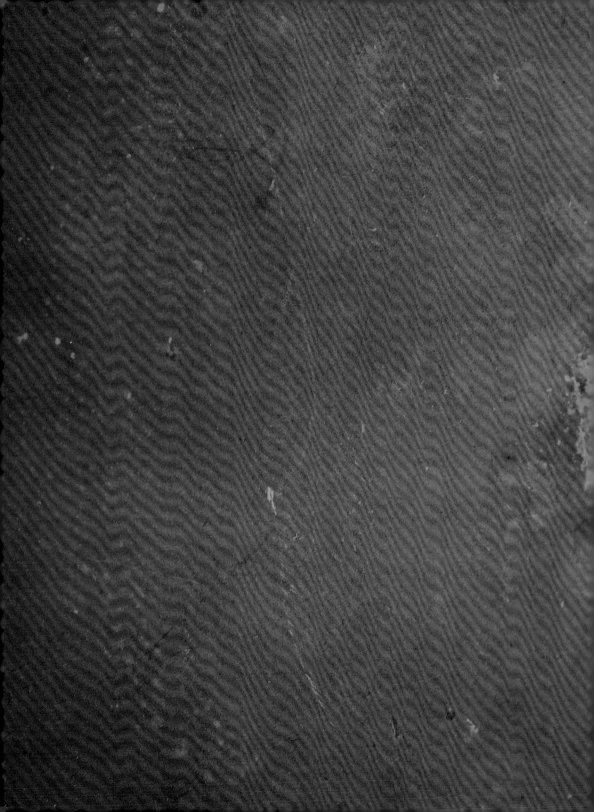

{ Flat Breads and Pizzas }

Sheet Pan Crackers

MAKES TWO 18- BY 13-INCH CRACKERS

Ingredients

2 ½ cups almond flour + extra for forming crust

1 tablespoon extra-virgin olive oil, plus extra for greasing

1 tablespoon honey

1 teaspoon baking powder

½ teaspoon table salt

½ cup warm water

2 teaspoons poppy, sesame, rye, and or flaxseed, coarse sea salt or kosher salt, for sprinkling

Preparation

1. Mix all the ingredients in a medium bowl until well combined. Grease cookie sheet and place the dough on it. Grease parchment paper and press greased side on dough until dough is the thickness of ¼ inch.

2. Adjust oven rack to the lower-middle position and heat the oven to 350° F.

3. Sprinkle with the seeds and coarse salt. Bake until golden brown, about 20 minutes, rotating the baking sheet halfway through baking.

4. Let the crackers cool on the baking sheet for at least 15 minutes, then break into large pieces and serve.

Oven-Baked Flatbread

Ingredients

2 ½ to 2 ¾ cups almond flour

¼ cup coconut milk

1 tablespoon olive oil plus more
    for greasing

2 teaspoons baking powder

2 teaspoons sugar

1 ½ teaspoons salt

2 tablespoons sesame seeds, melted
    coconut oil, for brushing, coarse sea
    salt or kosher salt, for sprinkling

Preparation

1. Preheat oven to 350° F. Grease a cookie sheet. In a medium bowl, mix all ingredients until a thick dough forms.
2. Divide dough into 4 equal portions (or 8, for smaller portions) and place on greased cookie sheet.
3. Grease hands with olive oil. Form each portion of dough into a round flatbread ½ inch thick by pressing dough on greased cookie sheet with greased hands. Arrange flatbreads on cookie sheet, evenly spaced. Bake for 10–15 minutes until golden brown, rotate cookie sheet after 7 ½ minutes.
4. Transfer the bread to a wire rack, brush lightly with melted coconut oil, season with coarse salt, and let cool for about 5 minutes; wrap the warm bread in a clean kitchen towel while repeating with the remaining bread. Serve.

Sweet Potato Rosemary Focaccia

MAKES ONE 18- BY 13-INCH FOCACCIA

Ingredients

1 medium sweet potato peeled and sliced into 1-inch thick chunks

3 ½ to 3 ¾ cups almond flour

½ to ¾ cup coconut flour

½ cup extra-virgin olive oil

3 ½ tablespoons baking powder

1 ¼ teaspoons table salt

2 tablespoons fresh rosemary, coarse salt or kosher salt, for sprinkling

extra olive oil for greasing baking sheet

Preparation

1. Bring the potato and 3 cups of water to a simmer in a small saucepan and cook until the potato is tender and can be easily pierced with a fork, about 10 minutes. Using a slotted spoon, transfer the potato to a small bowl. Measure out and reserve 1 cup of the hot potato cooking water; set aside to cool just until warm. When the potato is cool enough to handle, grate on the larger holes of a box grater.

2. Mix all dry ingredients in one bowl, whisk to combine.

3. Mix all wet ingredients (including grated sweet potato) in one bowl, whisk to combine.

4. Add wet ingredients to dry ingredients and mix well.

5. Adjust an oven rack to the lower middle position and heat the oven to 425° F. Dimple the dough with wet fingertips, then drizzle the remaining 1 tablespoon of oil and sprinkle with rosemary and coarse salt. Bake until focaccia becomes golden brown and crisp, 20 to 25 minutes, rotating the baking sheet halfway through baking.

6. Transfer the focaccia to a wire rack and let cool for 10 minutes, serve warm or at room temperature.

Sweet Potato Sage Focaccia

Makes One 18 x 13 Inch Flatbread

Ingredients

1 medium sweet potato peeled and sliced into 1-inch thick chunks.

3 ½ to 3 ¾ cups almond flour

½ to ¾ cup coconut flour

½ cup extra-virgin olive oil

3 ½ tablespoons baking powder

1 ¼ teaspoons table salt

2 tablespoons coarse salt or kosher salt, for sprinkling

1 tablespoon fresh sage

24 whole fresh sage leaves

Preparation

1. Bring the potato and 3 cups of water to a simmer in a small saucepan and cook until the potato is tender and can be easily pierced with a fork, about 10 minutes. Using a slotted spoon, transfer the potato to a small bowl. Measure out and reserve 1 cup of the hot potato cooking water; set aside to cool just until warm. When the potato is cool enough to handle grate on the larger holes of the box grater.

2. Mix all dry ingredients in one bowl, whisk to combine.

3. Mix all wet (including grated sweet potato) ingredients in one bowl, whisk to combine.

4. Add wet ingredients to dry ingredients and mix well.

5. Adjust an oven rack to the lower middle position and heat the oven to 425° F. Dimple the dough with wet fingertips, then drizzle the remaining 1 tablespoon of oil and sprinkle with sage and coarse salt. Press sage leaves into the dimples. Bake until focaccia becomes golden brown and crisp, 20 to 25 minutes, rotating the baking sheet halfway through baking.

6. Transfer the focaccia to a wire rack and let cool for 10 minutes, serve warm or at room temperature.

Sweet Potato, Black Olive, and Thyme Focaccia

Makes One 18- by 13-Inch Flatbread

Ingredients

1 medium sweet potato peeled and sliced into 1-inch thick chunks

3 ½ to 3 ¾ cups almond flour

½ to ¾ cup coconut flour

½ cup extra-virgin olive oil

3 ½ tablespoons baking powder

1 ¼ teaspoons table salt

2 tablespoons coarse salt or kosher salt, for sprinkling

1 teaspoon minced fresh thyme

24 black olives, pitted

Preparation

1. Bring the potato and 3 cups of water to a simmer in a small saucepan and cook until the potato is tender and can be easily pierced with a fork, about 10 minutes. Using a slotted spoon, transfer the potato to a small bowl. Measure out and reserve 1 cup of the hot potato cooking water; set aside to cool just until warm. When the potato is cool enough to handle, grate on the larger holes of the box grater.

2. Mix all dry ingredients in one bowl, whisk to combine.

3. Mix all wet ingredients (including grated sweet potato) in one bowl, whisk to combine.

4. Add wet ingredients to dry ingredients and mix well.

5. Adjust an oven rack to the lower-middle position and heat the oven to 425° F.

6. Dimple the dough with wet fingertips, and then drizzle the remaining 1 tablespoon of oil and sprinkle with thyme and coarse salt. Press black olives into the dimples. Bake until focaccia becomes golden brown and crisp, 20 to 25 minutes, rotating the need prior instruction on prepping the baking sheet and its size halfway through baking.

7. Transfer the focaccia to a wire rack and let cool for 10 minutes, serve warm or at room temperature.

Basic Pizza Dough

MAKES 2 POUNDS DOUGH, ENOUGH FOR TWO 14-INCH PIZZAS

Ingredients

4 to 4 ¼ cups almond flour

1 tablespoon baking powder

1 ½ teaspoons salt

2 tablespoons olive oil

1 ½ cups warm water

coconut oil for greasing the pizza pans

Preparation

1. Preheat oven to 400° F. Grease two, 14-inch round pizza pans with coconut oil.
2. Add flour, baking powder, and salt together in a bowl and whisk to combine. Add olive oil and warm water to the flour mixture and stir with a wooden spoon until well combined.
3. Turn the dough out onto the pizza pans. Press dough into a 12-inch circle and bake for 10–12 minutes or until firm but not crisp.

Quick Pizza Sauce

MAKES ABOUT 3 CUPS, ENOUGH FOR 3 LARGE PIZZAS

Ingredients

2 tablespoons extra-virgin olive oil

2 garlic cloves, minced

1 can crushed tomatoes or 15 ounces peeled tomatoes, processed until resembling crushed tomatoes

dried basil and oregano to taste (optional)

salt and pepper

Preparation

1. Cook the oil and garlic together in a medium saucepan over medium heat until sizzling and fragrant, about 30 seconds. Stir in tomatoes and simmer until sauce is thickened, about 15 minutes. Season with salt and pepper to taste. Add basil and/or oregano if using, mix well. Use on your favorite pizza. Store remainder in refrigerator for up to 5 days. Or freeze for up to 6 months.

Pesto Pizza

Makes Two 14-Inch Pizzas

Ingredients

2 pounds basic pizza dough (see Basic Pizza Dough recipe)
olive oil, for brushing
1 tomato, thinly sliced
⅛ cup sliced olives
⅔ cup pesto sauce

Pesto Sauce
2 cups packed fresh basil leaves
2 cloves garlic
¼ cup pine nuts
⅔ cup olive oil, divided
kosher salt and freshly ground black pepper to taste

Preparation
1. Prepare crust and press onto greased pizza pans. Bake for 8–12 minutes until firm but not crisp.
2. Remove the crusts from the oven and set aside.
3. For the Pesto Sauce: Combine the basil, garlic, and pine nuts in a food processor and pulse until coarsely chopped. Add ½ cup of the oil and process until fully incorporated and smooth. Season with salt and pepper. For immediate use, add all of the remaining oil and pulse until smooth.
4. Spread the pesto sauce over pizza crust and top with olives and tomato. Serve immediately.

To Make Ahead
The pesto sauce can be frozen. If freezing, transfer to an air-tight container and drizzle remaining oil over the top. Freeze for up to 3 months. Thaw and stir before using.

Aloha Pizza

MAKES TWO 14-INCH PIZZAS

Ingredients

2 pounds basic pizza dough (see Basic Pizza Dough recipe)

olive oil, for brushing

2 cups pizza sauce (see Quick Pizza Sauce recipe)

1 cup pineapple chunks

6 ounces bacon, cooked and crumbled

Preparation

1. Prepare the crust and press onto greased pizza pans. Bake for 8–12 minutes until firm but not crisp.
2. Remove the crusts from the oven and set aside.
3. Spread 1 cup pizza sauce over the crust, leaving a ½ inch border around the edge. Sprinkle 1 cup pineapple chunks and bacon.

Arugula and Prosciutto Pizza

MAKES TWO 14-INCH PIZZAS

Ingredients

2 pounds basic pizza dough (see Basic Pizza Dough recipe)

olive oil, for brushing

2 cups pizza sauce (see Quick Pizza Sauce Recipe)

4 ounces thinly sliced prosciutto

2 cups fresh arugula

Preparation

1. Prepare the crusts and press onto greased pizza pans. Bake for 8–12 minutes until firm but not crisp.
2. Remove the crusts from the oven and set aside.
3. Lightly brush the outer ½ inch edge of the dough with oil. Spread 1 cup pizza sauce over the crust, leaving a ½ inch border around the edge.
4. Top with 4 ounces thinly sliced prosciutto and sprinkle with 2 cups fresh arugula. Serve immediately.

Pizza Margherita

Serves 4 to 6

Ingredients

---

2 pounds basic pizza dough (see Basic Pizza Dough recipe)

Topping

1 can diced tomatoes

¼ cup chopped fresh basil

½ teaspoon palm sugar

1 small garlic clove, minced

¼ teaspoon table salt

¼ teaspoon olive oil for brushing and drizzling

coarse sea salt or kosher salt, for sprinkling

Preparation

1. Prepare crust and press onto greased pizza pans. Bake for 8–12 minutes until firm but not crisp.
2. Remove the crusts from the oven and set aside.
3. Lightly brush the outer ½ inch edge of the crust with oil. Spread ½ cup of tomato mixture over the crust, leaving a 1 ½-inch border around the edge.
4. Drizzle with about 1 teaspoon of oil and sprinkle with the remaining half of basil, garlic and coarse salt. Serve immediately.

Margherita Sheet Pan Pizza

MAKES ONE PIZZA

SERVES 12

Ingredients

Dough	Topping
4 ¾ to 5 cups almond flour	5 tablespoons olive oil, plus extra for brushing
5 tablespoons baking powder	3 garlic cloves, minced
1 tablespoon palm sugar	2 tablespoons tomato paste
2 teaspoons salt	28-ounce can crushed tomatoes
¼ cup olive oil + 2 tablespoons for greasing baking sheet and waxed paper	1 ½ teaspoons dried oregano
1 cup warm water	¼ teaspoon red pepper flakes
	2 tablespoons chopped fresh basil
	2 tablespoons salt to taste

Preparation

1. Adjust the oven rack to the lower-middle position and preheat the oven to 400° F. Coat an 18- by 13-inch baking sheet with the remaining ¼ cup oil.

2. For the sauce: Cook 1 tablespoon of the oil and the garlic together in a medium saucepan over medium heat until sizzling and fragrant, about 30 seconds. Stir in the tomato paste, oregano, and pepper flakes and cook, stirring often, until paste begins to boil, about 2 minutes. Stir in the crushed tomatoes and simmer until the sauce is thickened, about 10 minutes. Turn off the heat, stir in the basil and season with salt to taste.

3. For the dough: Add 4 ¾ cups of flour, baking powder, sugar, and salt to a large bowl and whisk to combine. Add olive oil and warm water to the flour mixture and stir with a wooden spoon until well combined.

4. Place dough on a greased baking sheet. Cut a piece of waxed paper the size of the baking sheet. Place waxed paper on counter and pour a small quantity of oil in the center of the paper. Using your fingers coat the entire surface of the waxed

paper. Press greased wax paper on dough and use to spread dough to an even thickness across the entire pan.

5. Place baking pan in oven and bake crust for 3–4 minutes, just until crust surface begins to dry and will tolerate spreading sauce on top without tearing.

6. Remove baking pan from oven and quickly spread tomato sauce over the dough, leaving a 1-inch border around the edge. Brush edge with olive oil. Bake until sauce darkens and steams. Remove from oven and top with olives, garlic, and chopped basil. Serve immediately.

Sausage and Pepperoni Sheet Pan Pizza

Ingredients

Dough

4 ¾ to 5 cups almond flour

5 tablespoons baking powder

1 tablespoon sugar

2 teaspoons salt

¼ cup olive oil

1 ¾ cups warm water

Topping

5 tablespoons olive oil, plus extra for
    brushing

3 garlic cloves, minced

2 tablespoons tomato paste oregano

1 ½ teaspoons dried oregano

¼ teaspoon red pepper flakes

2 tablespoons chopped fresh basil

2 tablespoons salt (or to taste)

1 pound browned sweet Italian sausage

3 ½ ounces thinly sliced deli pepperoni

Preparation

1. Adjust the oven rack to the lower-middle position and preheat the oven to 400°
    F. Coat 18- by 13-inch baking sheet with the remaining ¼ cup oil.

2. For the sauce: Cook 1 tablespoon of the oil and the garlic together in a medium
    saucepan over medium heat until sizzling and fragrant, about 30 seconds. Stir in
    the tomato paste, oregano, and pepper flakes and cook, stirring often, until paste
    begins to boil, about 2 minutes. Stir in the crushed tomatoes and simmer until
    the sauce is thickened, about 10 minutes. Turn off the heat, stir in the basil and
    season with salt to taste.

3. For the dough: Add 4 ¾ cups of flour, baking powder, sugar, and salt to a large
    bowl and whisk to combine. Add 1/4 cup of olive oil and warm water to the flour
    mixture and stir with a wooden spoon until well combined.

4. Place dough on a greased baking sheet. Cut a piece of waxed paper the size of the
    baking sheet. Place waxed paper on counter and pour 1 tablespoon of oil in the
    center of the paper. Using your fingers coat the entire surface of the waxed paper.

Press greased wax paper on dough and use to spread dough to an even thickness across the entire pan.

5. Place baking pan in oven and bake crust for 3–4 minutes, just until crust surface begins to dry and will tolerate spreading sauce on top without tearing.

6. Remove baking pan from oven and quickly spread tomato sauce over the dough, leaving a 1-inch border around the edge. Brush edge with olive oil. Sprinkle with browned sausage and pepperoni. Bake until sauce darkens and steams. Remove from oven and serve hot.

Sausage and Broccoli Rabe Sheet Pan Pizza

MAKES ONE PIZZA

SERVES 12

Ingredients

Dough
4 ¾ to 5 cups almond flour
5 tablespoons baking powder
1 tablespoon palm sugar
2 teaspoons salt
¼ cup olive oil
1 ¾ cups warm water

Topping
5 tablespoons olive oil, plus extra for
brushing

3 garlic cloves, minced
2 tablespoons tomato paste oregano
1 ½ teaspoons dried oregano
¼ teaspoon red pepper flakes
2 tablespoons chopped fresh basil
2 tablespoons salt (or to taste)
8 ounces Italian sausage, removed from
casings and browned
12 ounces broccoli rabe, cut into 1-inch
pieces

Preparation

1. Adjust the oven rack to the lower-middle position and preheat the oven to 400°
    F. Coat an 18- by 13-inch baking sheet with the remaining ¼ cup oil.
2. For the sauce: Cook 1 tablespoon of the oil and the garlic together in a medium saucepan
    over medium heat until sizzling and fragrant, about 30 seconds. Stir in the tomato paste,
    oregano, and pepper flakes and cook, stirring often, until paste begins to boil, about 2
    minutes. Stir in the crushed tomatoes and simmer until the sauce is thickened, about 10
    minutes. Turn off the heat, stir in the basil and season with salt to taste.
3. For the dough: Add 4 ¾ cups of flour, baking powder, sugar, and salt to a large
    bowl and whisk to combine. Add 1/4 cup of olive oil and warm water to the flour
    mixture and stir with a wooden spoon until well combined.
4. Place dough on a greased baking sheet. Cut a piece of waxed paper the size of
    the baking sheet. Place waxed paper on counter and pour 1 tablespoon of oil in
    the center of the paper. Using your fingers, coat the entire surface of the waxed
    paper. Press greased wax paper on dough and use to spread dough to an even
    thickness across the entire pan.
5. Place baking pan in oven and bake crust for 3–4 minutes, just until crust surface
    begins to dry and will tolerate spreading sauce on top without tearing.

6. Remove baking pan from oven and quickly spread tomato sauce over dough, leaving a 1-inch border around the edge. Brush edge with olive oil. Bake until sauce darkens and steams. Remove from oven and add topping.

7. For the topping: Brown the Italian sausage in a nonstick skillet over high heat, breaking it up with a wooden spoon. Add the broccoli rabe and 1 tablespoon water, stirring constantly until the rabe is crisp tender. Scrape mixture into a bowl and set aside. Sprinkle evenly over pizza sauce and bake until sauce is darkened.

8. Serve hot.

Veggie Delight Sheet Pan Pizza

MAKES ONE PIZZA

SERVES 12

Ingredients

Dough

4 ¾ to 5 cups almond flour

5 tablespoons baking powder

1 tablespoon palm sugar

2 teaspoons salt

¼ cup olive oil

1 ¾ cups warm water

Topping

5 tablespoons olive oil, plus extra for
  brushing

3 garlic cloves, minced

2 tablespoons tomato paste

1 ½ teaspoons dried oregano

¼ teaspoon red pepper flakes

28-ounce can crushed tomatoes

2 tablespoons chopped fresh basil

2 tablespoons salt (or to taste)

1 chopped and sautéed onion

1 red and 1 green bell pepper, seeded and
  chopped

10 ounces sliced white mushrooms and
  1 tablespoon vegetable oil

olive oil for sautéing vegetables

Preparation

1. Adjust the oven rack to the lower middle position and preheat the oven to 400°
   F. Coat an 18- by 13-inch baking sheet with the ¼ cup oil.

2. For the sauce: Cook 1 tablespoon of the oil and the garlic together in a medium
   saucepan over medium heat until sizzling and fragrant, about 30 seconds. Stir in
   the tomato paste, oregano, and pepper flakes and cook, stirring often, until paste
   begins to boil, about 2 minutes. Stir in the crushed tomatoes and simmer until
   the sauce is thickened, about 10 minutes. Turn off the heat, stir in the basil and
   season with salt to taste.

3. For the dough: Add 4 ¾ cups of flour, baking powder, sugar, and salt to a large
   bowl and whisk to combine. Add ¼ cup of olive oil and warm water to the flour
   mixture and stir with a wooden spoon until well combined.

4. Place dough on a greased baking sheet. Cut a piece of waxed paper the size of the
   baking sheet. Place waxed paper on counter and pour a small quantity of oil in

the center of the paper. Using your fingers coat the entire surface of the waxed paper. Press greased wax paper on dough and use to spread dough to an even thickness across the entire pan.

5. Place baking pan in oven and bake crust for 3–4 minutes, just until crust surface begins to dry and will tolerate spreading sauce on top without tearing.

6. Remove baking pan from oven and quickly spread tomato sauce over dough, leaving a 1-inch border around the edge. Brush edge with oil. Bake until sauce darkens and steams. Remove from oven and add topping.

7. In a nonstick skillet add olive oil, 1 chopped onion, 1 red and 1 green bell pepper, seeded and chopped, 10 ounces sliced white mushrooms and sauté until crisp tender.

8. Top pizza with sautéed vegetables. Serve hot.

Stromboli Sheet Pan Pizza

MAKES ONE PIZZA

SERVES 12

Ingredients

Dough

4 ¾ to 5 cups almond flour

5 tablespoons baking powder

1 tablespoon palm sugar

2 teaspoons salt

¼ cup olive oil

1 ¾ cups warm water

Topping

5 tablespoons olive oil, plus extra
    for brushing

3 garlic cloves, minced

2 tablespoons tomato paste

28-ounce can crushed tomatoes

1 ½ teaspoons dried oregano

¼ teaspoon red pepper flakes

2 tablespoons chopped fresh basil

2 tablespoons salt (or to taste)

4 ounces thinly sliced salami

4 ounces capocollo

½ cup of jarred roasted red bell peppers,
    rinsed, patted dry, and thinly sliced

Preparation

1. Adjust the oven rack to the lower-middle position and preheat the oven to 400° F. Coat an 18- by 13-inch baking sheet with the ¼ cup oil.

2. For the sauce: Cook 1 tablespoon of the oil and the garlic together in a medium saucepan over medium heat until sizzling and fragrant, about 30 seconds. Stir in the tomato paste, oregano, and pepper flakes and cook, stirring often, until paste begins to boil, about 2 minutes. Stir in the crushed tomatoes and simmer until the sauce is thickened, about 10 minutes. Turn off the heat, stir in the basil and season with salt to taste.

3. For the dough: Add 4 ¾ cups of flour, baking powder, sugar, and salt to a large bowl and whisk to combine. Add 1/4 cup olive oil and warm water to the flour mixture and stir with a wooden spoon until well combined.

4. Place baking pan in oven and bake crust for 3–4 minutes, just until crust surface begins to dry and will tolerate spreading sauce on top without tearing.

5. Spread the sauce evenly on the crust and add the sliced salami, capocolla, and red bell pepper slices. Bake until sauce darkens.

6. Serve hot

{ Rolls }

Dinner Rolls

Ingredients

1 ½ cups coconut milk

½ cup honey

7 tablespoons coconut oil, melted and cooled

2 large eggs

5 cups almond flour + ½ cup more if needed

5 tablespoons baking powder

2 teaspoons salt

coconut oil for greasing foil sling, hands, cutting board, and plastic wrap

Preparation

1. Preheat oven to 350° F. Grease a 15-muffin tin or a 24 mini-muffin tin.
2. Mix all wet ingredients: milk, eggs, coconut oil, and honey, in a medium bowl. Whisk to combine.
3. Mix all dry, remaining ingredients in a large bowl and whisk to combine. Add wet ingredients to dry ingredients and whisk to combine.
4. Pour equal quantities, ⅔ full, of batter into each muffin cup.
5. Place muffin tin into oven and bake for 15–17 minutes or until golden brown and firm. If not sure of doneness, insert a toothpick in center of one of the rolls and if it comes out clean, it's done. Rotate pan halfway through the baking time.
6. Place tin on cooling rack for 5 minutes. Remove rolls and serve warm.

Hearty Rustic Rolls

MAKES 12 ROLLS

Ingredients

20 ounces unroasted/raw cashews or cashew pieces or slivered almonds

½ cup filtered water

enough probiotic capsules to equal about 30-40 billion strains

4 large eggs, separated

2 tablespoons filtered water

1 teaspoon baking soda

½ teaspoon sea salt

coconut oil for greasing

Preparation

1. For the "sourdough" starter: In a food processor blend together the cashews or almonds and filtered water until **very** smooth. Stop and stir as needed to keep the mixture moving as it is quite thick. Be patient, this could take up to 10 minutes depending on your processor. You don't want it to be grainy. Transfer to a non-reactive bowl (such as glass or ceramic); add the probiotic powder and stir until well combined. The mixture will be thick.

2. Cover the bowl with a plate. Place it in the middle of your oven with the oven light on. Do NOT turn the oven on. The light will create a slightly warm environment and allow the probiotics to be active. Leave in oven for 12 to 20 hours—the longer it sits, the sourer it becomes. I make mine at 6 to 7 p.m. and bake the bread the next day at 11 a.m. to noon.

3. Preheat oven to 350° F.

4. Transfer the cashew or almond mixture to a larger bowl using a rubber spatula to transfer all of the nut starter.

5. Separate the egg yolks from the whites, putting the egg whites into a medium-sized bowl. Add salt, yolks, and 2 tablespoons of water to the cashew mixture and beat until smooth and lump free.

6. Rinse and dry the beaters so they're ready to beat the egg whites. Just before beating the egg whites, baking soda into the cashew mixture.

7. Using a hand mixer, beat the egg whites until soft peaks form. Gently fold them into the batter until the egg whites are no longer visible.

8. Grease a 12-cup muffin tin with coconut oil. Pour equal quantities of batter into each of the muffin cups, filling the cups ⅔ full. Place in oven and bake for 15–17 minutes at 350° F. They are done when a toothpick inserted comes out clean. Brush each roll with egg wash.

Hearty Rosemary Olive Rolls

MAKES 12 ROLLS

Ingredients

20 ounces unroasted/raw cashews or
    cashew pieces or slivered almonds
½ cup filtered water
enough probiotic capsules to equal about
    30-40 billion strains
4 large eggs, separated
2 tablespoons filtered water

1 teaspoon baking soda
½ teaspoon sea salt
1 cup pitted and sliced green or
    black olives
1 tablespoon minced fresh rosemary
coconut oil for greasing

Preparation

1. For the "sourdough" starter: In a food processor blend together the cashews or almonds and filtered water until **very** smooth. Stop and stir as needed to keep the mixture moving as it is quite thick. Be patient, this could take up to 10 minutes depending on your processor. You don't want it to be grainy. Transfer to a non-reactive bowl (such as glass or ceramic); add the probiotic powder and stir until well combined. The mixture will be thick.

2. Cover the bowl with a plate. Place it in the middle of your oven with the oven light on. Do NOT turn the oven on. The light will create a slightly warm environment and allow the probiotics to be active. Leave in oven for 12 to 20 hours—the longer it sits, the more sour it becomes. I make mine at 6 to 7 p.m. and bake the bread the next day at 11 a.m. to noon.

3. Preheat oven to 350° F.

4. Transfer the cashew or almond mixture to a larger bowl using a rubber spatula to transfer all of the nut starter.

5. Separate the egg yolks from the whites, putting the egg whites into a medium-sized bowl. Add the salt, rosemary, olives, yolks, and 2 tablespoons of water to the cashew mixture and beat until smooth and lump free.

6. Rinse and dry the beaters so they're ready to beat the egg whites. Just before beating the egg whites, baking soda into the cashew mixture.

7. Using a hand mixer, beat the egg whites until soft peaks form. Gently fold them into the batter until the egg whites are no longer visible.

8. Grease a 12-cup muffin tin with coconut oil. Pour equal quantities of batter into each of the muffin cups, filling the cups ⅔ full. Place in oven and bake for 15–17 minutes at 350° F. They are done when a toothpick inserted comes out clean. Brush each roll with egg wash.

Hearty Cranberry Pecan Rolls

Ingredients

20 ounces unroasted/raw cashews or cashew pieces or slivered almonds

½ cup filtered water

enough probiotic capsules to equal about 30-40 billion strains

4 large eggs, separated

2 tablespoons filtered water

1 teaspoon baking soda

½ teaspoon sea salt

1 cup pecans, toasted and coarsely chopped

¼ cup dried cranberries

coconut oil for greasing

Preparation

1. For the "sourdough" starter: In a food processor blend together the cashews or almonds and filtered water until **very** smooth. Stop and stir as needed to keep the mixture moving as it is quite thick. Be patient, this could take up to 10 minutes depending on your processor. You don't want it to be grainy. Transfer to a non-reactive bowl (such as glass or ceramic); add the probiotic powder and stir until well combined. The mixture will be thick.

2. Cover the bowl with a plate. Place it in the middle of your oven with the oven light on. Do NOT turn the oven on. The light will create a slightly warm environment and allow the probiotics to be active. Leave in oven for 12 to 20 hours—the longer it sits, the more sour it becomes. I make mine at 6 to 7 p.m. and bake the bread the next day at 11 a.m. to noon.

3. Preheat oven to 350° F.

4. Transfer the cashew or almond mixture to a larger bowl using a rubber spatula to transfer all of the nut starter.

5. Separate the egg yolks from the whites, putting the egg whites into a medium-sized bowl. Add the salt, yolks, and 2 tablespoons of water to the cashew mixture and beat till smooth and lump free.

6. Rinse and dry the beaters so they're ready to beat the egg whites. Just before beating the egg whites, baking soda, pecans and cranberries into the cashew mixture.

7. Using a hand mixer, beat the egg whites until soft peaks form. Gently fold them into the batter until the egg whites are no longer visible.

8. Grease a12-cup muffin tin with coconut oil. Pour equal quantities of batter into each of the muffin cups filling the cups ⅔ full. Place in oven and bake for 15–17 minutes at 350° F. They are done when a toothpick inserted comes out clean. Brush each roll with egg wash.

Hearty Chocolate Cherry Rolls

Ingredients

20 ounces unroasted/raw cashews or cashew pieces or slivered almonds

½ cup filtered water

enough probiotic capsules to equal about 30-40 billion strains

4 large eggs, separated

2 tablespoons filtered water

1 teaspoon baking soda

½ teaspoon sea salt

2 tablespoons cocoa powder

4 ounces nondairy bittersweet chocolate

¼ cup dried cherries

coconut oil for greasing

Preparation

1. For the "sourdough" starter: In a food processor blend together the cashews or almonds and filtered water until very smooth. Stop and stir as needed to keep the mixture moving as it is thick. Be patient, this could take up to 10 minutes depending on your processor. You don't want it to be grainy. Transfer to a non-reactive bowl (such as glass or ceramic); add the probiotic powder and stir until well combined. The mixture will be thick.
2. Cover the bowl with a plate. Place it in the middle of your oven with the oven light on. Do NOT turn the oven on. The light will create a slightly warm environment and allow the probiotics to be active. Leave in oven for 12 to 20 hours—the longer it sits, the more sour it becomes. I make mine at 6 to 7 p.m. and bake the bread the next day at 11 a.m. to noon.
3. Preheat oven to 350° F.
4. Transfer the cashew or almond mixture to a larger bowl using a rubber spatula to transfer all of the nut starter.
5. Separate the egg yolks from the whites, putting the egg whites into a medium-sized bowl. Add the salt, yolks, and 2 tablespoons of water to the cashew mixture and beat until smooth and lump free.
6. Rinse and dry the beaters so they're ready to beat the egg whites. Just before beating the egg whites, stir the salt, cocoa powder, chocolate, cherries and baking soda into the cashew mixture.
7. Using a hand mixer, beat the egg whites until soft peaks form. Gently fold them into the batter until the egg whites are no longer visible.
8. Grease a 12-cup muffin tin with coconut oil. Pour equal quantities of batter into each of the muffin cups, filling the cups ⅔ full. Place in oven and bake for 15–17 minutes at 350° F. They are done when a toothpick inserted comes out clean. Brush each roll with egg wash.

{ Sandwich Breads }

White Sandwich Bread

MAKES ONE 9-INCH LOAF

Ingredients

1 cup warm coconut milk

3 tablespoons coconut oil, melted and cooled

2 tablespoons honey

2 cups almond flour

1 ½ cups coconut flour and ½ cup extra if needed

1 tablespoon baking powder

2 teaspoons salt

extra coconut oil for greasing loaf pan.

Preparation

1. Preheat oven to 350° F. Grease a 9- by 5-inch loaf pan with coconut oil.
2. Mix all dry ingredients together in a bowl and whisk to combine.
3. Mix all wet ingredients together in a bowl and whisk to combine.
4. Add wet ingredients to dry ingredients in a bowl and whisk to combine.
5. Scrape the dough into the prepared loaf pan using a rubber spatula. Bake until golden brown, 20 to 30 minutes, rotating the loaf halfway through baking. Cool the loaf in the pan for about 15 minutes, then flip out onto a wire rack and let cool to room temperature, up to 2 hours before serving.

Hearty Sandwich Bread

MAKES ONE 9-INCH LOAF

Ingredients

1 cup warm coconut milk

3 tablespoons coconut oil, melted and cooled, plus 1 tablespoon extra for brushing

2 tablespoons honey

2 cups almond flour

1 ½ cups coconut flour and ½ cup extra if needed

1 tablespoon baking powder

2 teaspoons salt

2 tablespoons flaxseed

Preparation

1. Preheat oven to 350° F. Grease a 9- by 5- inch loaf pan with coconut oil.
2. Mix all dry ingredients together in a bowl and whisk to combine.
3. Mix all wet ingredients together in a bowl and whisk to combine.
4. Add wet ingredients to dry ingredients in a bowl and whisk to combine.
5. Scrape the dough into the prepared loaf pan using a rubber spatula. Bake until golden brown, 20 to 30 minutes, rotating the loaf halfway through baking. Cool the loaf in the pan for about 15 minutes, then flip out onto a wire rack and let cool to room temperature, up to 2 hours before serving.

Almond Meal Sandwich Bread

MAKES ONE 9-INCH LOAF

Ingredients

1 cup warm coconut milk

3 tablespoons coconut oil, melted and cooled, plus 1 tablespoon extra for brushing

2 tablespoons honey

1 ½ cups almond flour

½ cup almond meal

1 ½ cups coconut flour and ½ cup extra if needed

1 tablespoon baking powder

2 teaspoons salt

Preparation

1. Preheat oven to 350° F. Grease a 9- by 5-inch loaf pan with coconut oil.
2. Mix all dry ingredients together in a bowl and whisk to combine.
3. Mix all wet ingredients together in a bowl and whisk to combine.
4. Add wet ingredients to dry ingredients in a bowl and whisk to combine.
5. Scrape the dough into the prepared loaf pan using a rubber spatula. Bake until golden brown, 20 to 30 minutes, rotating the loaf halfway through baking. Cool the loaf in the pan for about 15 minutes, then flip out onto a wire rack and let cool to room temperature, up to 2 hours before serving.

Honey Sandwich Bread

Ingredients

¾ cup warm coconut milk

3 tablespoons coconut oil, melted and cooled, plus 1 tablespoon extra for brushing

¼ cup honey

2 cups almond flour

1 ½ cups coconut flour and ½ cup extra if needed

1 tablespoon baking powder

2 teaspoons salt

Preparation

1. Preheat oven to 350° F. Grease a 9- by 5-inch loaf pan with coconut oil.
2. Mix all dry ingredients together in a bowl and whisk to combine.
3. Mix all wet ingredients together in a bowl and whisk to combine.
4. Add wet ingredients to dry ingredients in a bowl and whisk to combine.
5. Scrape the dough into the prepared loaf pan using a rubber spatula. Bake until golden brown, 20 to 30 minutes, rotating the loaf halfway through baking. Cool the loaf in the pan for about 15 minutes, then flip out onto a wire rack and let cool to room temperature, about 2 hours before serving.

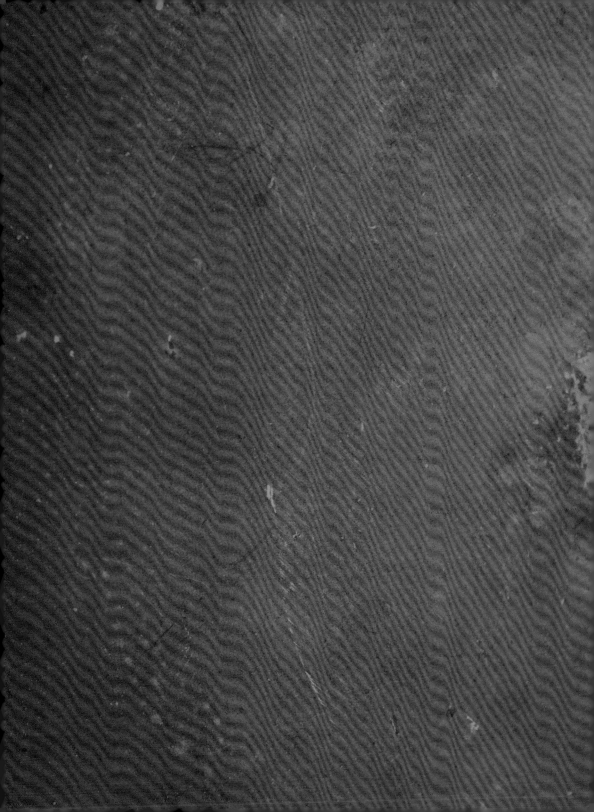

{ Artisan Breads }

"Sourdough" Cashew Bread

Makes One 9-Inch Loaf

Ingredients

10 ounces unroasted/raw cashews or cashew pieces

4 ounces filtered water

enough probiotic capsules to equal about 30-40 billion strains

2 large eggs, separated

1 tablespoon filtered water

½ teaspoon baking soda

¼ teaspoon sea salt

1 egg yolk plus 1 teaspoon water for egg wash

coconut oil for greasing the loaf pan

Preparation

1. For the "sourdough" starter: In a food processor blend together the cashews or almonds and filtered water until **very** smooth. Stop and stir as needed to keep the mixture moving as it is quite thick. Be patient, this could take up to 10 minutes depending on your processor. You don't want it to be grainy. Transfer to a non-reactive bowl (such as glass or ceramic); add the probiotic powder and stir until well combined. The mixture will be thick.

2. Cover the bowl with a plate. Place it in the middle of your oven with the oven light on. Do NOT turn the oven on. The light will create a slightly warm environment and allow the probiotics to be active. Leave in oven for 12 to 20 hours—the longer it sits, the sourer it becomes. I make mine at 6 to 7 p.m. and bake the bread the next day at 11 a.m. to noon.

3. Preheat oven to 350° F.

4. Transfer the cashew or almond mixture to a larger bowl using a rubber spatula to transfer all of the nut starter.

5. Separate the egg yolks from the whites, putting the egg whites into a medium-sized bowl. Add the salt, yolks, and 2 tablespoons of filtered water to the cashew mixture and beat until smooth and lump free.

6. Rinse and dry the beaters so they're ready to beat the egg whites. Just before beating the egg whites, stir the salt and baking soda into the cashew mixture.

7. Using a hand mixer, beat the egg whites until soft peaks form. Gently fold them into the batter until the egg whites are no longer visible.

8. Grease a 9- by 5-inch loaf pan with coconut oil. Pour batter into the pan. Place in oven and bake for 15 to 17 minutes at 350° F. The loaf is done when a toothpick inserted comes out clean. Brush each roll with egg wash.

Almond Sourdough Bread

MAKES ONE LOAF

Ingredients

10 ounces slivered almonds for completely starch-free

4 ounces filtered water

enough probiotic capsules to equal about 30-40 billion strains

2 large eggs, separated

1 tablespoon filtered water

½ teaspoon baking soda

¼ teaspoon sea salt

one egg yolk plus 1 teaspoon water for egg wash

You will need a 7.5- by 3.5-inch bread pan or one of equivalent size or double the recipe for a standard size loaf pan.

Preparation

1. For the "sourdough" starter: In a food processor blend together the almonds and filtered water until **very** smooth. Stop and stir as needed to keep the mixture moving as it is quite thick. Be patient, this could take up to 10 minutes depending on your processor. You don't want it to be grainy. Transfer to a nonreactive bowl (such as glass or ceramic); add the probiotic powder and stir until well combined. The mixture will be thick.

2. Cover the bowl with a plate. Place it in the middle of your oven with the oven light on. Do NOT turn the oven on. The light will create a slightly warm environment and allow the probiotics to be active. Leave in oven for 12 to 20 hours—the longer it sits, the sourer it becomes. I make mine at 6 to 7 p.m. and bake the bread the next day at 11 a.m. to noon.

3. Preheat oven to 350° F.

4. Transfer the almond mixture to a larger bowl using a rubber spatula to transfer all of the nut starter.

5. Separate the egg yolks from the whites, putting the egg whites into a medium-sized bowl. Add the salt, yolks, and 2 tablespoons of filtered water to the almond mixture and beat till smooth and lump free.

6. Rinse and dry the beaters so they're ready to beat the egg whites. Just before beating the egg whites, baking soda into the almond mixture.

7. Using a hand mixer, beat the egg whites until soft peaks form. Gently fold them into the batter until the egg whites are no longer visible.

8. Grease the loaf pan with coconut oil. Pour batter into the pan. Place in oven and bake for 15 to 17 minutes at 350° F. The loaf is done when a toothpick inserted comes out clean. Brush each roll with egg wash.

{ Breakfast and Brunch }

Classic Pancakes

MAKES ABOUT 16 PANCAKES

Ingredients

1 ½ cups almond flour

½ cup coconut flour

2 tablespoons palm sugar

2 teaspoons baking powder

½ teaspoon baking soda

½ teaspoon salt

2 cups coconut milk

2 teaspoons lemon juice

3 tablespoons unsalted coconut oil, melted
  and cooled

2 large eggs

1 teaspoon vanilla extract

coconut oil to grease the pan

Preparation

1. Adjust an oven rack to the middle position and heat the oven to 200° F. Set a wire rack over a baking sheet and place in oven for keeping pancakes warm.

2. Whisk the flours, palm sugar, baking powder, baking soda, and salt together in a large bowl. In a medium bowl, whisk the coconut milk, melted coconut oil, lemon juice, and eggs together. Make a well in the center of the flour mixture, pour the coconut milk mixture into the well, and gently whisk together just until incorporated with a few lumps remaining.

3. Heat a 12-inch nonstick skillet over medium heat for 3 to 5 minutes. Brush the pan bottom with a thin layer of the coconut oil. Using ¼ cup of batter per pancake, add the batter to the skillet and cook until large bubbles begin to appear.

4. Flip the pancakes and continue to cook until golden brown, about 1 ½ minutes. Transfer pancakes to the wire rack in the oven and keep warm. Repeat with remaining batter, brushing the skillet with oil as needed. Serve warm.

Blueberry Pancakes

Ingredients

1 ½ cups almond flour	2 teaspoons lemon juice
½ cup coconut flour	3 tablespoons unsalted coconut oil,
2 tablespoons palm sugar	melted and cooled
2 teaspoons baking powder	2 large eggs
½ teaspoon baking soda	1 teaspoon vanilla extract
½ teaspoon salt	coconut oil for the pan
2 cups coconut milk	1 cup blueberries

Preparation

1. Adjust an oven rack to the middle position and heat the oven to 200° F. Set a wire rack over a baking sheet and place in oven for keeping pancakes warm.

2. Whisk the flours, palm sugar, baking powder, baking soda, and salt together in a large bowl. In a medium bowl, whisk the coconut milk, melted coconut oil, lemon juice, vanilla, and eggs together. Make a well in the center of the flour mixture, pour the coconut milk mixture into the well, and gently whisk together just until incorporated with a few lumps remaining. Fold in blueberries to combine.

3. Heat a 12-inch nonstick skillet over medium heat for 3 to 5 minutes. Brush the pan bottom with a thin layer of the coconut oil. Using ¼ cup of batter per pancake, add the batter to the skillet and cook until large bubbles begin to appear.

4. Flip the pancakes and continue to cook until golden brown, about 1 ½ minutes. Transfer pancakes to the wire rack and keep warm in oven. Repeat with remaining batter, brushing the skillet with oil as needed. Serve warm.

German Apple Pancakes

SERVES 4

Ingredients

½ cup almond flour

½ tablespoon baking powder

1 tablespoon palm sugar

½ teaspoon salt

⅔ cup coconut milk

2 large eggs

1 teaspoon vanilla extract

2 tablespoons unsalted coconut oil

1 ¼ pounds apples, peeled, cored, quartered, and sliced ½ inch thick

¼ cup palm sugar

¼ teaspoon ground cinnamon

1 teaspoon fresh lemon juice

Preparation

1. Adjust an oven rack to the upper-middle position and heat the oven to 500° F. Whisk the flour, 1 tablespoon palm sugar, and salt together in a large bowl. In a small bowl, whisk the coconut milk, eggs, and vanilla together. Whisk the coconut milk mixture into the flour mixture until smooth with no lumps.

2. Melt the coconut oil in a 10-inch ovenproof nonstick skillet over medium-high heat. Add the apples, palm sugar, and cinnamon and cook, stirring often, until the apples are golden brown, about 10 minutes. Turn off the heat, stir in the lemon juice.

3. Quickly pour the batter around the edge of the skillet, then over the apples. Place the skillet in the oven and immediately reduce the oven temperature to 425° F. Bake until the pancake is brown and has risen above the edge of the skillet, about 18 minutes. Remove from oven and allow to stand 3 minutes before serving. Serve warm with or without maple syrup. Excellent served with a side of thick cut bacon.

French Toast

Ingredients

8 slices high quality paleo sandwich bread (see White Sandwich Bread recipe)

6 tablespoons unsalted coconut oil

1 ½ cups coconut milk

2 large eggs

2 tablespoons palm sugar

2 teaspoons vanilla extract

¾ teaspoon ground cinnamon

1 pinch ground nutmeg

¼ teaspoon salt

½ cup almond flour

Preparation

1. Adjust an oven rack to the middle position and heat the oven to 200° F. Arrange the bread on a wire rack, set over a baking sheet and bake until slightly dry, about 15 minutes. Remove bread from the rack and set aside. Repeat with remaining bread. Leave oven on and place wire rack on baking sheet and place back in the oven.

2. Meanwhile, melt 2 tablespoons of the coconut oil and whisk together with the milk, eggs, palm sugar, and vanilla, cinnamon, nutmeg, and salt in a medium bowl. Slowly whisk in the flour until smooth. Pour the batter into a large shallow dish.

3. Lay 2 pieces of dried bread in the batter and briefly soak both sides, about 30 seconds per side. Meanwhile melt one more teaspoon of coconut oil in a 12-inch nonstick skillet over medium heat, swirling to coat the pan.

4. Remove the bread from the batter, allowing excess batter to drip back into the dish, and lay in the hot skillet. Cook until golden brown on both sides, about 2 ½ minutes per side. Transfer the French toast to the wire rack and keep warm in the oven. Repeat with the remaining bread, coconut oil, and batter. Serve warm.

Stuffed French Toast

SERVES 4

Ingredients

6 ounces almond butter, softened

¼ cup palm sugar

¼ teaspoon ground cinnamon

pinch ground nutmeg

8 slices high quality paleo sandwich bread
(see White Sandwich Bread recipe)

4 tablespoons unsalted coconut oil

1 cup coconut milk

1 large egg

2 tablespoons vanilla extract

¼ teaspoon salt

½ cup almond flour

Preparation

1. Mix the almond butter, 2 tablespoons of palm sugar, cinnamon, and nutmeg together in a bowl until smooth.

2. Meanwhile, adjust an oven rack to the middle position and heat the oven to 200° F. Arrange the bread on a wire rack set over a baking sheet and bake until slightly dry, about 15 minutes; set aside, leaving the oven on. Line a second baking sheet with a wire rack; set aside.

3. Spread the almond butter mixture evenly over 4 pieces of bread, leaving a ½-inch border at the edges. Lightly press the remaining slices of bread over the top to make 4 sturdy sandwiches.

4. Melt 2 tablespoons of coconut oil and whisk together with the milk, egg, vanilla, salt, and remaining 2 tablespoons palm sugar in a medium bowl. Slowly whisk in the flour until smooth. Pour the batter into a large shallow dish.

5. Lay 2 sandwiches in the batter and soak both sides, about 1 minute per side. Meanwhile, melt 1 more tablespoon coconut oil in a 12-inch nonstick skillet over medium heat swirling to coat the pan.

6. Remove the bread from the batter, allowing the excess batter to drip back into the dish, and lay in the hot skillet. Cook until golden brown on both sides, about 2 ½ minutes per side. Transfer the French toast to the wire rack and keep warm in the oven. Repeat with the remaining sandwiches, coconut oil, and batter. Serve.

Apricot-Almond Stuffed French Toast

SERVES 4

Ingredients

6 ounces almond butter, softened

2 tablespoons apricot jam

⅛ teaspoon almond extract

pinch ground nutmeg

8 slices high quality paleo sandwich bread
  (see White Sandwich Bread recipe)

4 tablespoons coconut oil

1 cup coconut milk

1 large egg

2 tablespoons vanilla extract

¼ teaspoon salt

½ cup almond flour

Preparation

1. Mix the almond butter, 2 tablespoons of apricot jam, ⅛ teaspoon almond extract, and nutmeg together in a bowl until smooth.

2. Meanwhile, adjust an oven rack to the middle position and heat the oven to 200° F. Arrange the bread on a wire rack set over a baking sheet and bake until slightly dry, about 15 minutes; set aside, leaving the oven on. Line a second baking sheet with a wire rack; set aside.

3. Spread the almond butter mixture evenly over 4 pieces of bread, leaving a ½-inch border at the edges. Lightly press the remaining slices of bread over the top to make 4 sturdy sandwiches.

4. Melt 2 tablespoons of coconut oil and whisk together with the milk, egg, vanilla, salt, and remaining 2 tablespoons palm sugar in a medium bowl. Slowly whisk in the flour until smooth. Pour the batter into a large shallow dish.

5. Lay 2 sandwiches in the batter and soak both sides, about 1 minute per side. Meanwhile, melt 1 more tablespoon coconut oil in a 12-inch nonstick skillet over medium heat, swirling to coat the pan.

6. Remove the bread from the batter, allowing the excess batter to drip back into the dish, and lay in the hot skillet. Cook until golden brown on both sides, about 2 ½ minutes per side. Transfer the French toast to the wire rack and keep warm in the oven. Repeat with the remaining sandwiches, coconut oil, and batter. Serve.

Chocolate Chip-Stuffed French Toast

SERVES 4

Ingredients

4 ounces almond butter, softened

¼ cup palm sugar

¼ cup cacao nibs

8 slices high quality paleo sandwich bread
(see White Sandwich Bread recipe)

4 tablespoons coconut oil

1 cup coconut milk

1 large egg

2 tablespoons vanilla extract

¼ teaspoon salt

½ cup almond flour

Preparation

1. Mix the almond butter, 2 tablespoons of palm sugar, and cacao nibs together in a bowl until smooth.

2. Meanwhile, adjust an oven rack to the middle position and heat the oven to 200° F. Arrange the bread on a wire rack set over a baking sheet and bake until slightly dry, about 15 minutes; set aside, leaving the oven on. Line a second baking sheet with a wire rack; set aside.

3. Spread the almond butter mixture evenly over 4 pieces of bread, leaving a ½-inch border at the edges. Lightly press the remaining slices of bread over the top to make 4 sturdy sandwiches.

4. Melt 2 tablespoons of coconut oil and whisk together with the milk, egg, vanilla, salt, and remaining 2 tablespoons palm sugar in a medium bowl. Slowly whisk in the flour until smooth. Pour the batter into a large shallow dish.

5. Lay 2 sandwiches in the batter and soak both sides, about 1 minute per side. Meanwhile, melt 1 more tablespoon coconut oil in a 12-inch nonstick skillet over medium heat, swirling to coat the pan.

6. Remove the bread from the batter, allowing the excess batter to drip back into the dish, and lay in the hot skillet. Cook until golden brown on both sides, about 2 ½ minutes per side. Transfer the French toast to the wire rack and keep warm in the oven. Repeat with the remaining sandwiches, coconut oil, and batter. Serve.

Make ahead French Toast Casserole

Serves 6 to 8

Ingredients

Casserole

1 loaf paleo white sandwich bread
(page 173), sliced ½ inch thick

8 large eggs

2 cups coconut milk

1 tablespoon granulated palm sugar

2 teaspoons vanilla extract

½ teaspoon ground palm sugar

½ teaspoon ground nutmeg

Topping

12 tablespoons coconut oil, softened

1 ⅓ cups palm sugar

3 tablespoons honey

1 cup pecans, chopped coarse

Preparation

1. For the casserole: Adjust the oven racks to the upper-middle and lower-middle positions and heat the oven to 325° F. Arrange the bread in a single layer on 2 baking sheets. Toast in the oven until dry and lightly golden, about 25 minutes, switching and rotating the sheets halfway through baking. Set the bread aside to cool.

2. Grease a 13- by 9-inch baking dish. Layer the toasted bread tightly into the prepared dish. Whisk together the eggs, milk, coconut palm sugar, vanilla, cinnamon, and nutmeg and pour evenly over the bread. Press lightly on the bread to submerge.

3. Cover with plastic wrap and refrigerate for at least 8 hours or up to 24 hours. When ready to bake, adjust an oven rack to the middle position and heat the oven to 325° F.

4. For the topping: Mix the coconut oil, palm sugar, and honey together until smooth, then stir in the pecans. Spoon the topping over the casserole and spread it in an even layer. Place the dish on a rimmed baking sheet and bake until puffed and golden, about 60 minutes. Let cool slightly before serving. If excess oil is visible, drain it off before serving.

Make ahead Rum-Raisin French Toast Casserole

SERVES 6 TO 8

Ingredients

Casserole

1 loaf paleo white sandwich bread
(page 173), sliced ½ inch thick

8 large eggs

1 ½ cups coconut milk

1 tablespoon granulated palm sugar

2 teaspoons vanilla extract

½ teaspoon ground cinnamon

½ teaspoon ground nutmeg

1 ½ cups raisins

½ cup rum

Topping

12 tablespoons coconut oil, softened

1 ⅓ cups palm sugar

3 tablespoons honey

1 cup pecans, chopped coarse

Preparation

1. For the casserole: Adjust the oven rack to the upper-middle and lower-middle positions and heat the oven to 325° F. Arrange the bread in a single layer on 2 baking sheets. Toast in the oven until dry and lightly golden, about 25 minutes, switching and rotating the sheets halfway through baking. Set the bread aside to cool.

2. Grease a 13- by 9-inch baking dish. Layer the toasted bread tightly into the prepared dish. Microwave 1 ½ cups raisins and ½ cup rum together in a covered microwave-safe bowl on high until the rum comes to a boil, 1 to 3 minutes; set aside, covered, until the raisins are plump, about 15 minutes. Drain the raisins and sprinkle between the 2 layers of bread. Whisk together the eggs, coconut milk, palm sugar, vanilla, cinnamon, and nutmeg and pour evenly over the bread. Press lightly on the bread to submerge.

3. Cover with plastic wrap and refrigerate for at least 8 hours or up to 24 hours. When ready to bake, adjust an oven rack to the middle position and heat the oven to 325° F.

4. For the topping: Mix the coconut oil, palm sugar, and honey together until smooth, then stir in the pecans. Spoon the topping over the casserole and spread it in an even layer. Place the dish on a rimmed baking sheet and bake until puffed and golden, about 60 minutes. Let cool slightly before serving. If excess oil is visible, drain off before serving.

Quick Coffee Cake

MAKES TWO 9-INCH CAKES, EACH SERVING 6

Ingredients

Topping

⅔ cup palm sugar

⅓ cup almond flour

4 tablespoons coconut oil, softened

1 tablespoon ground cinnamon

1 cup pecans or walnuts, chopped coarse

Cake

2 cups almond flour

1 cup coconut flour

1 tablespoon baking powder

1 teaspoon baking soda

1 teaspoon ground cinnamon

¼ teaspoon salt

1 ¾ cups coconut milk

2 cups palm sugar

3 large eggs

7 tablespoons unsalted coconut oil, melted and cooled

Extra coconut oil for greasing pans

Preparation

1. Adjust an oven rack to the middle position and heat oven to 350° F. Grease two 9-inch cake pans.
2. For the topping: Using your fingers, mix the palm sugar, flour, coconut oil, and cinnamon together in a medium bowl until the mixture resembles wet sand. Stir in the pecans and set aside.
3. For the cake: Whisk the flours, baking powder, baking soda, cinnamon, and salt together in a large bowl. In a medium bowl, whisk the coconut milk, palm sugar, eggs, and melted coconut oil together until smooth. Gently fold the egg mixture into the flour mixture until smooth.
4. Scrape the batter into the prepared pans and smooth the top. Sprinkle the topping evenly over the top of both cakes.
5. Bake until the tops are golden and a toothpick inserted into the center comes out with just a few crumbs attached, 25 to 30 minutes, rotating the pan halfway through baking. Cool on a wire rack for 15 minutes before serving.

Quick Lemon-Blueberry Coffee Cake

Ingredients

Topping

⅓ cup packed light brown palm sugar

⅔ cup palm sugar

⅓ cup almond flour

4 tablespoons coconut oil, softened

1 tablespoon ground cinnamon

1 cup pecans or walnuts, chopped coarse

Cake

2 cups almond flour

1 cup coconut flour + 1 tablespoon for blueberries

1 tablespoon baking powder

1 teaspoon baking soda

1 teaspoon grated fresh lemon zest

2 cups fresh or frozen blueberries

1 teaspoon ground cinnamon

¼ teaspoon salt

1 ¾ cups coconut milk

2 cups palm sugar

3 large eggs

7 tablespoons coconut oil, melted and cooled

extra coconut oil for greasing pan

Preparation

1. Adjust an oven rack to the middle position and heat oven to 350° F. Grease two 9-inch cake pans.
2. For the topping: Using your fingers, mix both palm sugars, flour, coconut oil, and cinnamon together in a medium bowl until the mixture resembles wet sand. Stir in the pecans or walnuts and set aside.
3. For the cake: Whisk the flours, baking powder, baking soda, cinnamon, and salt together in a large bowl. Gently fold in 1 teaspoon grated fresh lemon zest and 2 cups fresh or frozen berries tossed with 1 tablespoon coconut flour. In a medium bowl, whisk the coconut milk, palm sugar, eggs, and melted coconut oil together until smooth. Gently fold the egg mixture into the flour mixture until smooth.
4. Scrape the batter into the prepared pans and smooth the top. Sprinkle the topping evenly over the top of both cakes.
5. Bake until the tops are golden and a toothpick inserted into the center comes out with just a few crumbs attached, 25 to 30 minutes, rotating the pan halfway through baking. Cool on a wire rack for 15 minutes before serving.

Quick Apricot-Orange Coffee Cake

MAKES TWO 9-INCH CAKES, EACH SERVING 6

Ingredients

Topping

⅔ cup sugar

⅓ cup almond flour

4 tablespoons coconut oil, softened

1 tablespoon ground cinnamon

1 cup pecans or walnuts, chopped coarse

Cake

3 cups almond flour

1 tablespoon baking powder

1 teaspoon baking soda

1 teaspoon ground cinnamon

¼ teaspoon salt

1 ¾ cups coconut milk

1 cup packed light brown palm sugar

1 cup granulated palm sugar

3 large eggs

7 tablespoons unsalted coconut oil, melted and cooled

1 teaspoon grated fresh orange zest

1 cup chopped dried apricots

extra coconut oil for greasing pans

Preparation

1. Adjust an oven rack to the middle position and heat oven to 350° F. Grease two 9-inch cake pans.
2. For the topping: Using your fingers, mix the palm sugar, flour, coconut oi, and cinnamon together in a medium bowl until the mixture resembles wet sand. Stir in the pecans or walnuts and set aside.
3. For the cake: Whisk the flour, baking powder, baking soda, cinnamon, and salt together in a large bowl. Gently fold in 1 teaspoon grated fresh orange zest and 1 cup chopped dried apricots. In a medium bowl, whisk the coconut milk, palm sugars, eggs, and melted coconut oil together until smooth. Gently fold the egg mixture into the flour mixture until smooth.
4. Scrape the batter into the prepared pans and smooth the top. Sprinkle the topping evenly over the top of both cakes.
5. Bake until the tops are golden and a toothpick inserted into the center comes out with just a few crumbs attached, 25 to 30 minutes, rotating the pan halfway through baking. Cool on a wire rack for 15 minutes before serving.

Quick Cranberry-Orange Cake

Makes Two 9-Inch Cakes, Each Serving 6

Ingredients

Topping

⅔ cup palm sugar

⅓ cup almond flour

4 tablespoons unsalted coconut oil, softened

1 tablespoon ground cinnamon

1 cup pecans or walnuts, chopped coarse

Cake

2 cups almond flour

1 cup coconut flour

1 tablespoon baking powder

1 teaspoon baking soda

1 teaspoon ground cinnamon

¼ teaspoon salt

1 ¾ cups coconut milk

2 cups palm sugar

3 large eggs

7 tablespoons coconut oil, melted and cooled

1 teaspoon grated fresh orange zest

1 cup dried cranberries

extra coconut oil for greasing pans

Preparation

1. Adjust an oven rack to the middle position and heat oven to 350° F. Grease two 9-inch cake pans.

2. For the topping: Using your fingers, mix the palm sugar, flour, coconut oi, and cinnamon together in a medium bowl until the mixture resembles wet sand. Stir in the pecans or walnuts and set aside.

3. For the cake: Whisk the flours, baking powder, baking soda, cinnamon, and salt together in a large bowl. Gently fold in the 1 teaspoon grated fresh orange zest and 1 cup dried cranberries. In a medium bowl, whisk the coconut milk, palm sugar, eggs, and melted coconut oil together until smooth. Gently fold the egg mixture into the flour mixture until smooth.

4. Scrape the batter into the prepared pans and smooth the top. Sprinkle the topping evenly over the top of both cakes.

5. Bake until the tops are golden and a toothpick inserted into the center comes out with just a few crumbs attached, 25 to 30 minutes, rotating the pan halfway through baking. Cool on a wire rack for 15 minutes before serving.

Almond Ring Coffee Cake

MAKES 2 RINGS, EACH SERVING 6

Ingredients

Topping
½ cup almond butter
¼ cup honey
¼ cup sliced almonds

Cake
2 cups almond flour
1 cup coconut flour
1 tablespoon baking powder

1 teaspoon baking soda
1 teaspoon ground cinnamon
¼ teaspoon salt
1 ¾ cups coconut milk
2 cups palm sugar
3 large eggs
7 tablespoons unsalted coconut oil, melted
    and cooled
Extra coconut oil for greasing pans

Preparation

1. Adjust an oven rack to the middle position and heat oven to 350° F. Grease tube pan.
2. For the topping: Place almond butter and honey in a small bowl and whisk until smooth. Microwave in 30 second intervals until liquid, stirring between intervals. Drizzle over cake and sprinkle sliced almonds over almond butter glaze. Serve warm.
3. For the cake: Whisk the flours, baking powder, baking soda, cinnamon, and salt together in a large bowl. In a medium bowl, whisk the coconut milk, palm sugar, eggs, and melted coconut oil together until smooth. Gently fold the egg mixture into the flour mixture until smooth.
4. Scrape the batter into the prepared pans and smooth the top. Sprinkle the topping evenly over the top of cakes.
5. Bake until the top is golden and toothpick inserted into the center comes out with just a few crumbs attached, 25 to 35 minutes, rotating the pan halfway through baking. Cool the cake on a wire rack for 15 minutes before glazing.

{ Flavored Maple Syrup and Jam }

Apple-Cinnamon Maple Syrup

Makes About 1 ¾ Cups

Ingredients

1 ½ cups maple syrup
⅓ cup finely diced apples
¼ teaspoon ground cinnamon
1 pinch of salt

Preparation

1. Simmer all the ingredients together in a small saucepan over medium low heat until slightly thickened, 5 to 7 minutes.

Berry Maple Syrup

Ingredients

½ cup frozen blueberries, strawberries, or raspberries

1 ½ cups maple syrup

¼ teaspoon grated fresh lemon zest

1 pinch of salt

Preparation

1. Cook the berries in a small saucepan over medium heat, mashing them constantly, until the moisture has evaporated, about 5 minutes. Whisk in the remaining ingredients, reduce the heat to medium low, and cook until slightly thickened, 5 to 7 minutes.

Paleo Fruit Jam

MAKES 1 PINT OR 8 OUNCES

Ingredients

3 cups frozen or fresh berries (choose one or a combination)

⅔ cup honey

juice of 1 lemon

Preparation

1. Place a small nonstick saucepan over medium heat.
2. Add berries and cook until they are thawed, hot, and juice begins to release from berries.
3. Add honey and lemon juice.
4. Using a wooden spoon, mix well and cook over medium heat for 7 minutes, then reduce heat and simmer for 7 more minutes. You may choose to simmer longer or shorter amount of time depending on the desired thickness. The longer you simmer, the thicker it will be.
5. Pack in a jar and seal with lid. Once the jam comes to room temperature, store in the refrigerator for up to 30 days.

{ Conversions and Equivalencies }

Ibelieve cooking is equal parts science and art, and your physical location has a lot to do with how to prepare a recipe. That is to say, the locations from which your ingredients originate have an impact on the overall recipe formulation. Ingredients from different parts of the world may vary slightly, and I cannot promise that almond flour from one supplier will yield exactly the same result as another. I can, however, offer guidelines for converting weights and measurements. I also recommend that you rely on your individual judgment (here's the art part) when preparing the recipes. If a recipe isn't behaving exactly as I describe it should, adjust the moisture, flours, or palm sugar levels until you get it right. The recipes in this book were developed using standard U.S. measures. The following charts offer equivalents for U.S., metric, and imperial (U.K.) measures. All conversions are approximate and have been rounded up or down to the nearest whole number.

EXAMPLE: 1 teaspoon = 4.9292 milliliters (rounded up to 5 milliliters)
1 ounce = 28.3495 grams (rounded down to 28 grams)

VOLUME CONVERSIONS U.S. TO METRIC

1 teaspoon = 5 milliliters	1¼ cups = 296 milliliters
2 teaspoons = 10 milliliters	1½ cups = 355 milliliters
1 tablespoon = 15 milliliters	2 cups (1 pint) = 473 milliliters
2 tablespoons = 30 milliliters	2½ cups = 591 milliliters
¼ cup = 59 milliliters	3 cups = 710 milliliters
⅓ cup = 79 milliliters	4 cups (1 quart) = 0.946 liter
½ cup = 118 milliliters	1.06 quarts = 1 liter
¾ cup = 177 milliliters	4 quarts (1 gallon) = 3.8 liters
1 cup = 237 milliliters	

VOLUME CONVERSIONS U.S. TO METRIC
Ounces To Grams

½ = 14	4½ = 128
¾ = 21	5 = 142
1 = 28	6 = 170
1½ = 43	7 = 198
2 = 57	8 = 227
2½ = 71	9 = 255
3 = 85	10 = 283
3½ = 99	12 = 340
4 = 113	16 (1 pound) = 454

OVEN TEMPERATURES: FAHRENHEIT TO CELSIUS AND TO GAS MARK (IMPERIAL)

225 = 105 = ¼

250 = 120 = ½

275 = 135 = 1

300 = 150 = 2

325 = 165 = 3

350 = 180 = 4

375 = 190 = 5

400 = 200 = 6

425 = 220 = 7

450 = 230 = 8

475 = 245 = 9

Subtract 32° F from the Fahrenheit reading, and then divide the result by 1.8 to find the Celsius reading.

Temperature conversion example:

175° F − 32 = 143°

143° ÷ 1.8 = 79.44° C, rounded down to 79° C

{ Recipe Index }